GHAZALS OF GHALIB

Ghazals of *Ghalib*

VERSIONS FROM THE URDU BY

Aijaz Ahmad, W.S. Merwin,
Adrienne Rich, William Stafford,
David Ray, Thomas Fitzsimmons,
Mark Strand, and William Hunt

Edited by
Aijaz Ahmed

OXFORD
UNIVERSITY PRESS

OXFORD
UNIVERSITY PRESS

Oxford University Press is a department of the University of Oxford.
It furthers the University's objective of excellence in research, scholarship,
and education by publishing worldwide. Oxford is a registered trademark of
Oxford University Press in the UK and in certain other countries

Published in India by
Oxford University Press
YMCA Library Building, 1 Jai Singh Road, New Delhi 110001, India

First published in 1991 by Columbia University Press
First Indian Edition in Oxford India Paperbacks 1994
Fifteenth impression 2011

ISBN-13: 978-0-19-563567-6
ISBN-10: 0-19-563567-1

Printed in India by Sapra Brothers, New Delhi 110 092

EDITOR'S NOTE

THE LITERAL TRANSLATIONS included in this book were done mainly from *Deevan-i-Ghalib* (Urdu), edited by Imtiyaz Ali Arshi (Aligarh, 1958) and the only really dependable edition of Ghalib's Urdu poetry. Other editions have been consulted but found not always trustworthy.

The limited scope of this book precludes any exhaustive discussion of Ghalib's life, so it is suggested that the interested reader consult *Yadgar-i-Ghalib* by Altaf Hussain Hali (Lucknow, 1932), which remains the most important source on the early life of Ghalib. However, Hali's critical opinions must be read in the light of his own taste for didactic and pragmatic writing. For any real sense of Ghalib's later life, his own letters are an indispensable and fortunately delightful source. Among the more modern scholarship, S. M. Ikram's work is by far the most rewarding. Nothing nearly so good has been done thus far in English.

It is impossible, and even pointless, to mention all the dictionaries one reads in the course of one's love affair with a language, or that one consults in the more limited course of a project such as the one represented by this book. However, I would like to add a few words of caution. First of all, no Urdu dictionary compiled during the last fifty years is of any real value; recent Urdu lexicography is a sad affair. Second, it is always prudent to consult Persian dictionaries when reading Ghalib; he often uses words of Persian origin with their original Persian meaning rather than, or in addition to, the adapted Urdu meanings of the same words. And, finally, I should like to emphasize that John T. Platt's *Dictionary of Urdu and Classical Hindi* is still the best Urdu-English dictionary for translating, particularly from nineteenth-century works.

As for the interpretive notes which appear at the end of my literal versions of couplets, I have, of course, read the usual scholarly commentaries, but only with a view to formulating what is finally my own understanding and response. Wherever interpretations by others have seemed to me to be unsatisfactory I have simply ignored them. In a book which is essentially a book of translations, and not a critique of the Ghalib criticism, this appeared to be entirely appropriate. Besides, literal translations and commentaries which would make most sense to my American collaborators needed different methods and points of emphasis than would have been the case had I been writing a commentary in Urdu primarily for an Urdu audience. My versions have that deliberate slant.

I wish to thank the Asian Literature Program of The Asia Society of New York for the initial grant which made this work possible. I thank, in particular, Mrs. Bonnie R. Crown, who inspired the work, saw it grow many times larger than it was first supposed to have been, and helped me in all ways so that I could do quite freely what I felt needed to be done. Thanks are due also to the staff of the Asian Literature Program for typing, retyping, Xeroxing, and re-Xeroxing the almost monumental mass of material from which this book has been shaped. I am indebted also to my friend, C. M. Naim of Chicago University, for many valuable suggestions. I should, however, single out Carolyn Kizer, to whom my debts are many and without whose selfless interest and assistance none of this would have ever been done.

A. A.

INTRODUCTION

THE SEVEN DECADES of Ghalib's life (1797–1869) were not a very auspicious time for the writing of poetry for anyone who lived in the city of Delhi. The British conquest of India was completed during those decades, the fabric of the entire civilization came loose, and the city of Delhi became a major focal point for countless traumatic crises. Ghalib was not, in the modern sense, a political poet—not political, in other words, in the sense of a commitment to strategies of resistance. Yet, surrounded by constant carnage, Ghalib wrote a poetry primarily of losses and consequent grief; a poetry also of what was, what could have been possible, but was no longer. In sensibility, it is a poetry somewhat like Wallace Stevens': meditative, full of reverberations, couched in a language at once sparkling and fastidious, and testifying to a sensibility whose primary virtue was endurance in a world that was growing for him, as for many others of his time and civilization, increasingly unbearable. The journey from nothingness to a totally human affirmation which is the essential growth of a poet of that tradition—beyond time, beyond the merely spatial relations—was achieved in his case with a necessary and austere urgency related, finally, to the experience of having been possessed. He is a tragic poet.

(I)

Mirza Asadullah Beg Khan—known to posterity as Ghalib, a *nom de plume* he adopted in the tradition of all classical Urdu poets—was born in the city of Agra, of parents with Turkish aristocratic ancestry, probably on December 27th, 1797. As to the precise date, Imtiyaz Ali Arshi has conjectured, on the basis of Ghalib's horoscope, that the poet might have been born a month later, in January 1798.

Both his father and uncle died while he was still very young, and he spent a good part of his early boyhood with his mother's family. This, of course, began a psychology of ambivalences for him. On the one hand, he grew up relatively free of any oppressive dominance by adult, male father-figures. This, it seems to me, accounts for at least some of the independence of spirit he showed from very early childhood. On the other hand, this placed him in the humiliating situation of being socially and economically dependent on maternal grandparents, giving him, one can surmise, a sense that whatever worldly goods he received were a matter of charity and not legitimately his. His preoccupation in later life with finding secure, legitimate, and comfortable means of livelihood can perhaps be at least partially understood in terms of this early uncertainty.

The question of Ghalib's early education has often confused Urdu scholars. Although any record of his formal education that might exist is extremely scanty, it is also true that Ghalib's circle of friends in Delhi included some of the most eminent minds of his time. There is, finally, irrevocably, the evidence of his writings, in verse as well as in prose, which are distinguished not only by creative excellence but also by the great knowledge of philosophy, ethics, theology, classical literature, grammar, and history that they reflect. I think it is reasonable to believe that Mulla Abdussamad Harmuzd —the man who was supposedly Ghalib's tutor, whom Ghalib mentions at times with great affection and respect, but whose very existence he sometimes denies—was, in fact, a real person and an actual tutor of Ghalib when Ghalib was a young boy in Agra. Harmuzd was a Zoroastrian from Iran, converted to Islam, and a devoted scholar of literature, language, and religions. He lived in anonymity in Agra while tutoring Ghalib, among others.

In or around 1810, two events of great importance occurred in Ghalib's life: he was married into a well-to-do, educated family of nobles, and he left for Delhi. One must remember that Ghalib was only thirteen at the time. It is impossible to say when Ghalib started writing poetry. Perhaps it was as early as his seventh or eighth years. On the other hand, there is evidence that most of what we know as his complete works were substantially completed by 1816, when he was 19 years old, and six years after he first came to Delhi. We are obviously dealing with a man whose maturation was both early and rapid. We can safely conjecture that the migration from Agra, which had once been a capital but was now one of the many important but declining cities, to Delhi, its grandeur kept intact by the existence of the Moghul court, was an important event in the life of this thirteen-year-old, newly married poet who desperately needed material security, who was beginning to take his career in letters seriously, and who was soon to be recognized as a genius, if not by the court at least by some of his most important contemporaries. As for the marriage, in the predominantly male-oriented society of Muslim India no one could expect Ghalib to take that event terribly seriously, and he didn't. The period did, however, mark the beginnings of the concern with material advancement that was to obsess him for the rest of his life.

In Delhi Ghalib lived a life of comfort, though he did not find immediate or great success. He wrote first in a style at once detached, obscure, and pedantic, but soon thereafter he adopted the fastidious, personal, complexly moral idiom which we now know as his mature style. It is astonishing that he should have gone from sheer precocity to the extremes of verbal ingenuity and obscurity, to a style which, next to Meer's, is the most important and comprehensive style of the ghazal in the Urdu language before he was even twenty.

The course of his life from 1821 onward is easier to trace. His interest began to shift decisively away from Urdu poetry to Persian during the 1820s, and he soon abandoned writing in Urdu almost altogether, except whenever a new edition of his work was forthcoming and he was inclined to make changes, deletions, or additions to his already existing opus. This remained the pattern of his work until 1847, the year when he gained direct access to the Moghul court. I think it is safe to say that throughout these years Ghalib was mainly occupied with the composition of Persian verse, with the preparation of occasional editions of his Urdu works which remained essentially the same in content, and with various intricate and exhausting proceedings undertaken with a view to improving his financial situation, these last consisting mainly of petitions to patrons and governments, including the British. Although very different in style and procedure, Ghalib's obsession with material means, and the accompanying sense of personal insecurity which seems to threaten the very basis of selfhood, reminds one strongly of Baudelaire. There is, through the years, the same self-absorption, the same overpowering sense of terror which comes when material want is experienced as moral hurt, the same effort to escape from the necessities of one's own creativity and intelligence, the same illusion—never really believed viscerally—that if one could be released from need one could perhaps become a better artist. There is the same flood of complaints, and finally the same triumph of a self which is at once morbid, elegant, highly creative, and almost doomed to realize the terms not only of its desperation but also its distinction.

Ghalib was never really a part of the court except in its very last years, and even then with ambivalence on both sides. There was no love lost between Ghalib himself and Zauq, the king's tutor in the writing of poetry; and if their mutual dislike was not often openly expressed, it was as a matter of prudence only. There is reason to believe that Bahadur Shah Zafar, the last Moghul king, and himself a poet of considerable merit, did not much care for Ghalib's style of poetry or life. There is also reason to believe that Ghalib not only regarded his own necessarily subservient conduct in relation to the king as humiliating but that he also considered the Moghul court a redundant institution. Nor was he well-known for admiring the king's verses. However, after Zauq's death Ghalib did gain an appointment as the king's advisor on matters of versification. He was also appointed, by royal order, to write the official history of the Moghul dynasty, a project which was to be titled *Partavistan* and to fill two volumes. The one volume, *Mehr-e-NeemRoz*, which Ghalib completed is an indifferent work, and the second volume was never completed, supposedly because of the great disturbances created by the Revolt of 1857 and the consequent termination of the Moghul rule. Possibly Ghalib's own lack of interest in the later Moghul kings had something to do with it.

The only favorable result of his connection with the court between 1847 and 1857 was that he resumed writing in Urdu with a frequency not experienced since the early 1820s. Many of these new poems are mere panegyrics, or occasional verses to celebrate this or that. He did, however, write many ghazals which are of the same excellence and temper as his early, great work. In fact, it is astonishing that a man who had more or less given up writing in Urdu thirty years before should, in a totally different time and circumstance, produce work that is, on the whole, neither worse nor better than his earlier work. One wonders just how many great poems were permanently lost to Urdu when Ghalib chose to turn to Persian instead.

In its material dimensions, Ghalib's life never really took root and remained always curiously unfinished. In a society where almost everybody seems to have had a house of his own, Ghalib never had one and always rented or accepted the use of one from a patron. He never had books of his own, usually reading borrowed ones. He had no children; the ones he had died in infancy, and he later adopted the two children of Arif, his wife's nephew who died young in 1852. Ghalib's one wish, perhaps as strong as the wish to be a great poet, that he should have a regular, secure income, never materialized. His brother, Yusuf, went mad in 1826 and died, still mad, in that year of all misfortunes, 1857. His relations with his wife were, at best, tentative, obscure, and indifferent. Given the social structure of mid-nineteenth-century Muslim India, it is, of course, inconceivable that *any* marriage could have even begun to satisfy the moral and intellectual intensities that Ghalib required from his relationships; given that social order, however, he could not conceive that his marriage could possibly serve that function. And one has to confront the fact that the child never died who, deprived of the security of having a father in a male-oriented society, had looked for material but also moral certainties—not certitudes, but certainties, something that he can stake his life on. So, when reading his poetry it must be remembered that it is the poetry of a more than usually vulnerable existence.

It is difficult to say precisely what Ghalib's attitude was toward the British conquest of India. The evidence is not only contradic-

tory but also incomplete. First of all, one has to realize that na-
tionalism as we know it today was simply nonexistent in nine-
teenth-century India. Second, one has to remember—no matter how
offensive it is to some—that, even prior to the British, India had a
long history of invaders who created empires which were eventually
considered legitimate. The Moghuls themselves were such invaders.
Given these two facts, it would be unreasonable to expect Ghalib
to have a clear ideological response to the British invasion. There is
also evidence, quite clearly deducible from his letters, that Ghalib
was aware, on the one hand, of the redundancy, the intrigues, the
sheer poverty of sophistication and intellectual potential, and the
lack of humane purposes of the Moghul court, and, on the other,
of the powers of rationalism and scientific progress of the West.

Ghalib had many attitudes toward the British, most of them com-
plicated and often quite contradictory. His diary of 1857, the *Dast-
Ambooh* [1] is a pro-British document, criticizing the British here and
there for excessively harsh rule but expressing, on the whole, horror
at the tactics of the resistance forces. His letters, however, are some
of the most graphic and vivid accounts of British violence that we
possess. We know also that *DastAmbooh* was always meant to be a
document that Ghalib would make public, not only to the Indian
Press but specifically to the British authorities. And he even wanted
to send a copy of it to Queen Victoria. His letters are, to the con-
trary, written to people he trusted very much, people who were his
friends and would not divulge their contents to the British author-
ities. As Imtiyaz Ali Arshi [2] has shown (at least to my satisfaction),
whenever Ghalib feared that the intimate, anti-British contents of
his letters might not remain private, he requested their destruction,
as he did in the case of his letters to the Nawab of Rampur. I think
it is reasonable to conjecture that the diary, the *Dast-Ambooh*, is
a document put together by a frightened man who was looking for
avenues of safety and forging versions of his own experience in order

[1] First published, in the original Persian, at Agra, 1858. Urdu translation, by
Makhmur Saidi, published in a magazine, *Tehrik*, Delhi, April–May, 1961.
[2] *Makateeb-e-Ghalib*, ed. Imtiyaz Ali Arshi, Rampur, 1937.

to please his oppressors, whereas the letters, those private documents of one-to-one intimacy, are more real in their expression of what Ghalib was in fact feeling at the time. And what he was feeling, according to the letters, was horror at the wholesale violence prac-ticed by the British.

Yet, matters are not so simple as that either. We can not explain things away in terms of altogether honest letters and an altogether dishonest diary. Human and intellectual responses are more com-plex. The fact is also that Ghalib, like many other Indians of the time, admired British, and therefore Western, rationalism as ex-pressed in constitutional law, city planning, and more. His trip to Calcutta (1828–29) had done much to convince him of the immedi-ate values of Western pragmatism. This immensely curious and hu-man man from the narrow streets of a decaying Delhi had suddenly been flung into the broad, well-planned avenues of 1828 Calcutta—from the aging Moghul capital to the new, prosperous, and clean capital of the rising British power, and, given the precociousness of his mind, he had not only walked on clean streets, but had also asked fundamental questions about the sort of mind that planned that sort of city. In short, he was impressed by much that was British.

In Calcutta he saw cleanliness, good city planning, prosperity. He was fascinated by the quality of the Western mind which was rational and could conceive of constitutional government, republicanism, skep-ticism. The Western mind was attractive particularly to one who, although fully imbued with his feudal and Muslim background, was also attracted by a wider intelligence like the one that West-ern scientific thought offered: good rationalism promised to be good government. The sense that this very rationalism, the very mind which had planned the first modern city in India, was also in the service of a brutal and brutalizing mercantile ethic which was to produce not a humane society but an empire, began to come to Ghalib only when the onslaught of 1857 caught up with the Delhi of his own friends. Whatever admiration he had ever felt for the British was seriously brought into question by the events of that year, more particularly by the mercilessness of the British in their dealings with those who participated in or sympathized with the Revolt. This is no place to go into the details of the massacre; I will refer here only to the recent researches of Dr. Ashraf,[3] in India, which prove that at least 27,000 persons were hanged during the summer of that one year in Delhi. Ghalib witnessed it all. It was obviously impossible for him to reconcile this conduct with whatever humanity and progressive ideals he had ever expected the British to have possessed. His letters tell of his terrible disaffection.

Ghalib's ambivalence toward the British possibly represents a characteristic dilemma of the Indian—indeed, the Asian—peoples. Whereas they are fascinated by the liberalism of the Western mind and virtually seduced by the possibility that Western science and technology might be the answer to poverty and other problems of their material existence, they feel a very deep repugnance for forms and intensities of violence which are also peculiarly Western. Ghalib was probably not as fully aware of his dilemma as the intellectuals of today might be; to assign such awareness to a mid-nineteenth-century Indian mind would be to violate it by denying the very terms—which means limitations, as well—of its existence. His bewilderment at the extent of the destruction caused by the very people of whose humanity he had been convinced can, however, be understood in terms of this basic ambivalence.

The years between 1857 and 1869 were neither happy nor very eventful ones for Ghalib. During the Revolt itself, Ghalib remained pretty much confined to his house, undoubtedly frightened by the wholesale massacres all over the city. Many of his friends were hanged, deprived of their fortunes, exiled from the city, or detained in jails. By October, 1858, he had completed his diary of the Revolt, the *DastAmbooh*, published it, and presented copies of it to the British authorities, mainly with the purpose of proving that he had not supported the insurrections. Although his life and immediate possessions were spared, little value was attached to his writings; he was flatly told that he was still suspected of having had loyalties

---

[3] Ashraf, K. M., "Ghalib & The Revolt of 1857," in *Rebellion 1857*, ed., P. C. Joshi. Delhi, 1957.

toward the Moghul king. During the ensuing years, his main source of income continued to be the stipend he got from the Nawab of Rampur. *Ud-i-Hindi,* the first collection of his letters, was published in October, 1868. Ghalib died a few months later, on February 15th, 1869.

(II)

In order to place Ghalib in his true context, one should perhaps first speak briefly of his language and tradition. In the initial stages of its growth, Urdu represents an amalgam of the medieval languages of Northern India—Bhasha, Khari Boli, and others—and languages of the Middle East, mainly Persian, which the Muslims brought with them. Thus, it is written in the Persianized form of the Arabic script, is syntactically based on a combination of Persian and Prakrit grammatical structures, and draws its highly flexible and assimilative vocabulary from a variety of Indo-European languages. The Persian element, however, has been dominant, to the extent that the entire body of traditional Urdu poetics—prosody, poetic forms, concepts relating to poetic diction and subject—have been almost wholly Persian. We can safely say that, from its beginnings in the fifteenth century until the latter half of the nineteenth, it was part of the larger Persian-Indic tradition. It is only in the closing decades of the nineteenth century that Urdu begins to assimilate Western forms and concepts through the growing influence of English throughout the subcontinent.

Like Persian, Urdu is also very much a language of abstractions. In this sense, it is very difficult to translate from Urdu into English. The movement in Urdu poetry is always *away* from concreteness. Meaning is not expressed or stated; it is signified. Urdu has only the shoddiest tradition of dramatic or descriptive poetry. The main tradition is one of highly condensed, reflective verse, with abundance and variety of lyrical effects, verbal complexity, and metaphorical abstraction. And this preference for abstractions is not, as should be obvious, merely a characteristic of language, but is also a way of thinking—of reflecting on man's place in the universe and his relations with the world, with others, with God, with his own interiority. Thus, although always a poetry of love, Urdu poetry, in its classical phase, never contemplates the experience of love in terms of a specific love relation. Specification and personality are kept rigorously out of the poetic substance.

The metaphysics of Urdu poetry, and of Ghalib in particular, can be approached in terms of three questions: What is the nature of the universe and man's place in it? What is God? What is love? For the Urdu poet, as for the Persian, these questions are interdependent. There is no question of clarifying man's place in the universe without first contemplating the nature of God, or of love. Similarly, there can be no poetry of love unless love is understood, first, as a human reflection of a divine possibility and, second, as a definition of man's place in his moral universe. Ghalib does not offer a celebration of love, or longing, or ecstasy, as mystic poets do. Except in some places, his is not normally a poetry of mystic disciplines; rather, it is a poetry of contemplation, making subtle, and if possible, precise distinctions between one experience and another, and various shades of each. Thus love is defined not once or twice but over and over again, so that a whole collection of couplets may signify the complexity involved.

As we have already said, the main body of Urdu poetics has been borrowed from the Persian. At the center of these poetics is the form of the ghazal, the basic poetic form in Urdu from the beginnings of the language to the middle of this century. The ghazal is a poem made up of couplets, each couplet wholly independent of any other in meaning and complete in itself as a unit of thought, emotion, and communication. No two couplets have to be related to each other in any way whatever except formally (one may be about love, the next about the coming of a season; one about politics, the next about spring), and yet they can be parts of a single poem. The *only* link is in terms of prosodic structure and rhymes. All the lines in a ghazal have to be of equal metrical length. The first is a rhymed couplet, and the second line of each succeeding couplet must rhyme with the opening couplet. The unit of rhyme repeated at the end of each couplet may be as short as a single syllable or as long as a phrase of half a line. The convention is that a ghazal should have at least five couplets. Otherwise it is considered a fragment. There is no maximum length.

It should be obvious that this form, based on two lines of equal length as a self-sufficient unit of poetry, is the product of the abstract nature of the language itself, and in turn reinforces the same character. Only when a unit of poetry is meant to communicate a single thought or emotion, and only when the poet sets out to deal with just the essence rather than the many particulars of an experience, can one have so small a unit and dispense with the idea of continuity. Within these expectations, the ghazal functions with an easily identifiable and almost repetitious pattern of imagery—the rose, the tulip, the nightingale, the seasons, a handful of descriptions of this or that, human or extra-human states—as does Japanese poetry, in which a certain flower, a certain time of day, even the plunge of a stone, can signify something other than itself.

(III)

Good poetic translations, like good poetry itself, are very much a matter of luck: talent, skill, and labor have all to be blessed with the divine spark. The problem is, of course, one of revealing the *whole* of the original mind by transferring to another language not only what it is saying, but also how it is saying whatever it says. Success can only be relative; the translator is in an impossible situation and translations of poetry can be not only rarely but also relatively good.

The problem of translating poetry from an Asian language is that the best translators of an age are its poets, but there is hardly a major poet in America today who knows even one of the languages of Asia well enough to translate from it without substantial, even decisive assistance from a native speaker of the language. This problem is further complicated by the contradictions within the environment

in which translations from Asian languages are usually undertaken.
I believe that the present is—next perhaps only to the Elizabethan
—a great age of translation in the English language, particularly
by the American poets. Yet something has clearly gone wrong: there
are too many *academic* translations. A labor which needs to be,
and rarely is, a labor of love is being undertaken on a vast scale and
being accomplished with deadening efficiency.

In presenting Ghalib to American readers, our foremost commit-
ment has been to a book of translations—versions, adaptations, imi-
tations, or whatever else one calls them—which is, above all, a book
of poetry. In such an enterprise, it is absolutely essential that the
finished versions be done by persons who are primarily poets and
not necessarily scholars of Urdu. This could, of course, be achieved
through collaboration only between an Urdu writer (in this case, my-
self) and several gifted American poets who have experience in work-
ing with raw, literal versions.

The editor determined that we should publish, within one volume,
the materials which were first given to the poets (literal versions,
lexical notes, etc.) as well as the finished poetic versions. Further,
we determined to print more than one version of single poems, pro-
vided that each finished version was a good poem in English and
dealt with the original material in an interesting or revealing fashion.
Although some good versions have had to be omitted for lack of
space, we have tried to incorporate within one volume as many al-
ternative versions as possible, not in order to conduct some kind of
a tournament, but in order to face one of the essentials of our under-
taking: given the fact that more than one poet had chosen to work
with the same body of materials, it was inevitable that we would
get more than one approach and more than one version of a given
poem which was really good. It was part of our original purpose
to get a multiplicity of responses, rather than one response, to
Ghalib, and we had started, from the outset, with the premise that
there *is* no one right way of translating a poem: one translation may
capture what another misses and both be, in different ways, good
translations. This book proposes one thing—only one: translation is

approximation. Perhaps the way out is that we strive for more than one inspired approximation, not by accident, but by design. Together, all these versions may, it is hoped, create an intense impression of Ghalib's mind and moral universe.

The present design is dictated by the editor's conviction that scholarship can best serve its own purposes by acknowledging its limitations, and that translations of poetry, though based on scholarship, have to have a poetic pulse that transcends the limits of what a scholar can ever accomplish. For example, the ghazals in these versions are almost always unrhymed; if rhymed, they are usually not restricted to any formal scheme. The fact is that formal devices, such as rhymed couplets or closely scannable prosodic structures are, in contemporary English as opposed to nineteenth-century Urdu, restrictive rather than enlarging or intensifying devices. The organic unity of the ghazal, as translated into English, does not depend on formal rhymes. Inner rhymes, allusions, verbal associations, wit, and imagistic relations can quite adequately take over the functions performed by the formal end-rhymes in the original Urdu.

The Urdu poet, and his Perisan counterpart even more, has suffered not only from neglect but also from the wrong kind of attention. By the time the British settled down in their colonies and areas of influence securely enough to start dabbling with the native literary traditions, the nineteenth century was well on its way. This tradition of translation has suffered fatally from the fact that the first conspicuous translations were done by people who came in contact with Urdu and Persian because of their involvement with matters and consequence of the Empire; by people who were not poets themselves, nor, with the exception of Fitzgerald, even men of imagination. They knew very little about poetry and worked with a poetic ideal derived from a post-Romantic, Tennysonized jargon in which, as Pound once noted, the same adjectives were used for women and sunsets. For these gentlemen of the Empire, poetry was essentially a substitute for daydreams and candy: twilit, sumptuous, escapist, and, finally, trivial. It was the pedants' attempt to turn out something sweet. Soon enough, even worse happened. With the British take-over of the educational system, Indians were themselves alienated from their own language and were brought up on huge chunks of Tennyson, Swinburne, Macaulay, Pater, and others. By the beginning of this century there were numerous Indians who considered Ghalib both the greatest poet of Urdu that ever lived and a sort of native Tennyson. The complex, the apocalyptic, and the moral were carefully sifted out in favor of a post-Romantic grief that fed upon itself, a synthetic nostalgia that had nothing whatever to do with the concrete stresses of public and private history that Ghalib suffered. If he wasn't already a Victorian Romanticist, he had to be made into one; if the tradition of Urdu poetry wasn't already minor or trivial, the design of the Empire demanded that triviality be imposed upon it. For decades major Urdu poets were being read according to standards set by minor English ones.

Out of all this bungling, there has emerged an image of the Persian and Urdu poets which is hard to undo: that of an amoral, epicurean poet eternally sitting under a tree with his woman, his loaf of bread, and his jug of wine. It is characteristic that Omar Khayyam, rather than Firdausi or Rumi or Hafiz, should be the best-known Persian poet in the West; it is characteristic that Khayyam's own reputation should be based on a translation which is Victorian and in fact very much an English poem of the Victorian temper; and, finally, it is characteristic that Robert Graves, the only major English poet who has so far addressed himself to Persian poetry, should return to the well-known *Rubaiyat* and· not to much greater Persian poets, like Hafiz and Rumi, whose work lies buried under uninspired and unreadable translations. I give these illustrations from Persian because Persian poetry has been more widely—if not better—translated into English, and because Classical Persian and Classical Urdu are related to each other in the same way as Old English and modern English are related; and Hafiz is to Ghalib roughly what Chaucer is to Shakespeare. Good translations should now aim at a revaluation which will finally show that, far from being epicurean or, as has often been said, a "poetry of roses and nightingales," the tradition of poetry that reaches its first greatness with Hafiz and Rumi in Persia and ends its Classical phase with Ghalib in Delhi is, at its best and in its own altogether different terms, as complex and moral as, for instance, the tradition of poetry from Chaucer to Berryman in English.

Needless to add that the scope of a book such as this can hardly begin to attempt a full portrait of an entire tradition. On the contrary, the aim here is very modest indeed. It is to present in good, readable translations a very few poems of a poet who is close enough to us in time but, in language and poetic form, is as remote from the West as Hafiz or Basho; a poet who lived at a time when his civilization was breaking up and who tells us what it was like to have lived and loved at a time which, at least so far as he was concerned, seemed to be the end of history. Of course, in order to hear what he has to tell us, we shall have to learn his language—by which I do not mean the Urdu language, but his sense of what words are all about, his sense and use of poetic form, and, above all, his sense of poetry in relation to the time in which it is written.

(IV)

Ghalib lived at a time in the history of the subcontinent similar to the present in America, in the sense that a whole civilization seemed to be breaking up and nothing of equal strength was taking its place. Worse still, what replaced the older civilization ran altogether counter to what Ghalib stood for. For a Muslim poet-intellectual who lived within the older order, life was difficult but intrinsically intelligible, being supported by a tradition within which he could confront and contain experience: there was a religion which he might or might not have observed in external detail and ritual but which certainly gave him a sense of contact with his God and the universe God had created; there were shared experiences and shared concepts of love, anxiety, friendship, and all the other emotions that define man's place in society; there was, in short, much suffering in that society but also a sense of relation and, finally, a sense that the poet lived in essential harmony with, not opposition to, his society. By the beginning of the nineteenth century, however, this sense of order was already going and the civilization was in serious doubt about its own validity: the British trader had assured that the old order was simply not worth preserving. It was at this moment of almost cosmic self-doubt in the subcontinental consciousness that Ghalib grew up and started writing. The seventy or so years of his life are the years when these self-doubts about civilization grew into final despair. There is in Ghalib a moral grandeur, as in Hafiz, but also an intense moral loneliness, a longing for relations which were no longer possible, and a sense of utter waste. To illustrate, I quote here the following four couplets, from four different ghazals, translated for this volume by Adrienne Rich:

> I am neither the loosening of song nor the close-drawn tent
> of music;
> I'm the sound, simply, of my own breaking.

and:

> Our time of awareness is a lightning-flash
> a blinding interval in which to know and suffer.

and:

> The dew has polished the sheen of the flowering branch.
> The nights of spring are finished, nightingale.

and, finally:

> I'm too old for an inner wildness, Ghalib,
> when the violence of the world is all around me.

In addition to this despair, there is, of course, a sense of tradition as well, a great longing for it and for a human contact possible only for a man who decides to live at all costs within human community. Take, for instance, the following couplets from a ghazal translated by William Stafford:

> Held behind lips, lament burdens the heart; the drop
> held to itself fails the river and is sucked into dust.

If you live aloof in the world's whole story,
the plot of your life drones on, a mere romance.

Either one enters the drift, part and whole as one,
or life is a mere game: Be, or be lost.

All these themes, and many more, come together with an inter-play of wonderfully concise images in a freer translation by W. S. Merwin of a ghazal that I quote in part:

The heart is burnt out
but its sufferings were nothing to yours
            oh my cry

                charred dove
                nightingale still burning

Worse than any fire fed by what was
was the fire of longing for what was not
                nothing was left of the spirit
                but the heart's suffering

Love holds him
prisoner he says
and something has him sealed

            like a great rock on his hand

Sun who turn everything into day
shine here too

a strange time
has come upon us like a shadow

This is a poetry of intense moral privacies; and of love—not *about* love, but *of* love. Love is the great, over-arching metaphor because love is conceived as the basic human relation and all life is lived in terms of this relation—even when those terms are terms of failure. And, finally, it is a poetry of reflections, in every sense of that term. Like a mirror within a mirror, each couplet is related to every other, and each reflects a situation that has been lived and reflected upon.

The Western poet most similar to Ghalib is perhaps Wallace Stevens. All the poems taken together create a single, intense impression of a life lived in fact and in mutual relations of facts, in the mind as much as in the imagination; and everything that enters the life also enters, in one way or another, into the poetry of that life. The chronology of the poems—what poem was written when, under what impulse—is far less important than the inner relations. For a poet like Ghalib—and for all the great Urdu poets, really—time does not happen in sequences, but in a sort of circular motion: immediate grief becomes a part of total grief, the poem written at sixteen enters into the poem written at sixty, all poems become parts of a single poem which, in turn, signifies the morality of a single mind.

As I have said, it is a poetry of moral privacies: moral and private. Everything that happens to the poet, either personally or to the times in which he lives, is deeply related to his poetry, but the immediate event is kept scrupulously out of that poetry. The response is immediate and moral, but the urgency is assimilated within privacy, and the response, as it is expressed in poetry, is not so much to the event as to the consequences of that event, to the way it has altered the poet, the experience of the poet. Ghalib undercuts the whole debate which proceeds from an assumption that the particular and the universal are, in some way, in opposition. For Ghalib, the particular *is* the universal: a man's history is the history of his intelligence, *plus* his emotions, *plus* his times. The image of man Ghalib posits is very much a matter of what man makes of his emotions. Again, this too is like the work of Wallace Stevens, where the Romantic and the rational are in a hard, terrifying, victorious embrace.

Like Stevens, Ghalib trusts the intelligence of his readers and makes demands on it. And he demands patience. He expects that you will read all his couplets together, that you will let these couplets sink into your consciousness, and will let them reveal themselves to you gradually, over the years. He expects that you will read these couplets as impressions of a man who sought wholeness at a time when wholeness was difficult—as it always is, but more so. Also, a man who needed love, knew it, knew its failures, yet sought for it always—in himself, and in his loveless times. Ghalib was a man who wrote poetry because poetry was necessary; the times were inauspicious and poetry alone had the power to save whatever could be saved in a portrait of man that was fast disappearing. Ghalib's poetry is a work of restoration on that portrait.

(V)

I cannot say in what terms Ghalib's poetry is relevant to our times, or to English. I don't know in what sense poetry is *ever* relevant. We are presenting only a segment of the whole, only thirty-seven out of the hundreds of ghazals—and in translation. A remote set of conventions in a poetry we have never, or almost never, read before can be formidable and forbidding, as Pakistani readers of American poetry and American readers of, say, Japanese poetry have discovered in the past. No amount of explaining can do the job. The only aid I can provide here is a passage from a letter Adrienne Rich wrote to me soon after beginning to work on these translations:

The marvelous thing about these ghazals is precisely (for me) their capacity for both concentration and a gathering, cumulative effect. . . . I needed a way of dealing with very complex and scattered material which was demanding a different kind of unity from that imposed on it by the isolated, single poem: in which certain experiences needed to find both their intensest rendering and to join with other experiences not logically or chronologically connected in any obvious way. I've been trying to make the couplets as autonomous as possible and to allow the unity of the ghazal to emerge from underneath, as it were, through images, through associations, private and otherwise. . . . For me, the couplets work only when I can keep them from being too epigrammatic; what I'm trying for, not always successfully, is a clear image or articulation behind which there are shadows, reverberations, reflections of reflections. In other words, something that will not remind the Western reader of haiku or any other brief, compact form, such as Pope's couplet in English, or the Greek anthology.

The poets who worked on these translations were free to choose their own methods. They were asked to be true only to the *spirit* of Ghalib's poetry; they could be literal, if they thought that was desired, or simply drift away from the strict accuracy of details in a given couplet or ghazal. As a result, we have here a true multiplicity of methods. Some poets, like Adrienne Rich and William Stafford, are brilliantly close to the original—without cluttering their versions with archaisms as literal translators of Urdu poetry tend to do, keeping clear of the trite, preserving quite wonderfully the intensity of Ghalib. Others, chiefly William Hunt and David Ray, have drifted quite far from any strict engagements with the details of the original. W. S. Merwin started working in couplets, with scrupulous attention to literal accuracy. But, somewhere along the line, he reverted to a method closer to his own poetry, stripping the image to its essentials, looking at the concrete object with unwavering and sometimes fierce attention, creating through economy of objects and language a poetry of reverberations, a sort of inner rhythm, and of constant possibility. And so, speaking through several voices and methods, we have discovered *our* Ghalib. In the process, we lost some, and found much. That, I think, is a risk in poetry, and one of its chief glories.

The responsibility for selecting ghazals, as well as the couplets in each ghazal, rests entirely with myself. I would like to note, however, that we did not set out to translate all that is representative or worth translating in Ghalib's work. Limitations of space made it inevitable that we settle for a much smaller cross-section of the work: a mere thirty-seven ghazals. Other than the limitations of space, this selection has been influenced by considerations of translatability and the editor's taste. I must confess that this taste was severely tested. In putting together his final opus, Ghalib had eliminated most of what lacked excellence; to make a further selection, and such a small one at that, can be frustrating.

The part of the process of selection which might attract special attention is that in practically all cases I have selected five or six couplets from within a ghazal. The principles applied here are the same as used in selecting the ghazals: space, translatability, my own taste. In addition, there are precedents. It is common practice in the subcontinent that whenever selections are made from a poet of the ghazal form he is represented by the best couplets of his ghazals. Similarly, when singers sing ghazals they often limit themselves to three or five couplets. And, it takes little knowledge of Urdu culture to realize that when the people of that culture memorize or recite poetry, as they do all the time, they recite couplets, not entire ghazals.

More recently, a case has been made, mainly by some Western orientalists, that the ghazal form has a circular unity of theme quite comparable to the Western concept of linear thematic unity. My acceptance of such a notion is quite conditional. First of all, the theory seems to have come out of a study of Hafiz, and what is common knowledge in Persia seems to be presented now as news: that Hafiz, unlike many other ghazal poets, tried to observe thematic associations in all couplets of his ghazal. This, however, applies neither to Ghalib nor to other poets of Urdu. Some ghazals of Ghalib do indeed have thematic unity; such ghazals are given here in their entirety.

Some explanation regarding the function and form of the literal versions is perhaps necessary. The reader should bear in mind the fact that the literal versions were made strictly for use by my American co-translators, and not originally for publication. As a result, they have the appearance of being raw, unfinished, somewhat chaotic. For instance, explanations for particular couplets or notes on vocabulary have been provided only sporadically. Where literal translations were seen as being self-evident, no further explanation was felt to be necessary. In deciding to make them available to the readers of this book, we have had to resist the temptation of cleaning them up and giving them more formal an appearance than they originally had. The intention is, again, to demonstrate a process, to let the reader see for himself precisely what went on in the process of collaboration.

I feel particularly happy in editing this book. Collaboration was always candid, easy, and enjoyable, and in several cases quite close. When we started planning these translations, we had in mind only a sort of Ghalib centennial pamphlet. The response from the poets who collaborated on translations was, however, enthusiastic and immediately gratifying, not only in their readiness to work but also in their quite astonishing perceptions. The book began to grow, and there were months when we did not even know how big a book we were finally going to have. I have been moved by the openness of various poets in accepting and even soliciting criticism, and by their readiness to do no less than their best. For this exposure, and their trust, I am grateful.

Aijaz Ahmad

Westhampton, Long Island
April 15, 1970

NOTE: I have tried to keep the literal translations as informal and readable as possible. The following key should help explain the method.

'a' is used as the u-sound in 'but'

'ā' is used as in 'wash'; 'ạ' is used for the a-sound as in 'bad'

'ai' as in 'train'

'Ay' or 'Aiy' are used for sounds approximating the sound one gets in 'flying' or 'dying'

'e', 'ee', 'i', 'o', 'oa', 'oo' have retained their normal sounds as in 'set,' 'seen,' 'bit,' 'hot,' 'boat' and 'roo'

'u' is always used as in 'put'

As for the consonants,

'd' is always soft

'd' is hard, as is normal in English words such as 'hard'

'g' is always hard

'gh' is, strictly speaking, not an English sound at all; pronounced from further back in the mouth, it is more like a French 'r'

'g̱h' means that both letters have to be pronounced separately and normally, with a hard 'g'

'n' is the normal English sound of that letter as in 'noun'

'ñ' is the nasal sound that occurs in such French names as 'Jean' or 'Villon'

'kh' is to be pronounced as a single sound, as in the German pronunciation of 'Bucharest'

'ph' means that the two letters have to be pronounced separately and normally; the f-sound which is obtained in English by combining these letters ('phantasy') is expressed here by 'f' alone

'q' is a 'k' pronounced very far back in the mouth

'r' is the normal English 'r'

'ṛ' is an 'r' pronounced further back in the mouth

't' is soft

'ṭ' is hard, as is normal in English

'th' is not the normal English sound, as in 'the'; the two letters have
   to be pronounced separately; the 't' is soft

NOTE FOR THE
PAPERBACK EDITION, 1994

Ghalib is, among all the Urdu poets, doubtless the most cunning. One approaches him, therefore, at *any* point in one's life, with much trepidation. The novelty of method in this book came from the conviction, already strong when I was still unforgivably young, that the pleasures of his poetry are largely untranslatable, more than poetry usually is. One could attempt at best not verisimilitude but a *range* of responses from very different kinds of contemporary sensibilities, so as to forge some analogues for Ghalib's own civilities and sentiments, and thereby retrieve, in idioms alien to him, perhaps a rumour of what those intensities were like. The exercise was difficult; so, poets that we were, we chose to be playful. But a reprint, almost a quarter century later, of a work that so smacks of the impetuosities of youth involves for me a different, more dreary set of embarrassments. In the intervening years, my views have changed about everything that has a bearing on my own role in this book: the Urdu language and its poetics; the place of Ghalib in our literary and intellectual histories; my understanding of those histories as such; not to speak of poetry itself. Most things in the Introduction, and some in the apparatus I then provided for my collaborators, now strike me as wrong.

A certain fondness for that collaboration remains, however, and the book includes many poems — *English* poems — of astonishing beauty and economy; quite a few manage an uncommonly profound relation with Ghalib. That is the main justification for this reprint and the reason why I have resisted the temptation to tinker with any of it. I resisted the idea of a re-issue for some years because I kept imagining that I would one day write a second Introduction, but I have had to keep attending to other needs. May there be yet another time when I can settle this debt!

Work on this book brought me the gift of Adrienne Rich's friendship. So, I should like to dedicate this re-print to that friendship, with those words of Charles Olson which she quoted in her own book of those years: 'what does not change/ Is the will to change.'

New Delhi
15 January 1994

ACKNOWLEDGEMENTS

Ten versions by Adrienne Rich and ten by William Stafford originally appeared in 'Poems by Ghalib', a special Ghalib Centennial booklet published by *The Hudson Review*, copyright © 1969 by The Hudson Review, Inc. The same poems appeared in *The Hudson Review*, Volume XXII, Number 4, Winter, 1969–70.

The following versions by W. S. Merwin first appeared in *Poetry*, August-September 1970, copyright © 1970 by Modern Poetry Association: 'There is only one beloved face'; 'Alright it's not love it's madness'; 'Flame is not so wonderful nor has the lightning'; 'If you were frail of heart'; 'Where I'm going is farther at every step'; If it ever occurs to her to be kind to me'; 'There are a thousand desires like this, each needing a lifetime'; 'It is a long time since my love stayed with me here.'

The literal and poets' versions of three ghazals appeared originally in a special Ghalib issue of *Mahfil*, Volume V, No. 4, 1968–69. William Stafford's version first appeared in *The Hudson Review's* Ghalib Centennial Booklet, 'Poems by Ghalib'. Printed with permission of *The Hudson Review*.

The literal and poets' versions of six ghazals appeared originally in *Delos*, No. 5, 1970, reprinted with the permission of the University of Texas at Austin.

Versions by Thomas Fitzsimmons, David Ray, William Stafford, and Mark Strand first appeared in *The Mahalat Review*, Number 14, April 1970.

Two versions by David Ray originally appeared in *Transpacific*, Volume II, No. 5, 1970.

The numbering system of the ghazals has been changed since magazine publication.

GHAZALS OF GHALIB

GHAZAL

❀ I ❀

دہر، جز جلوۂ یکتائیِ معشوق نہیں
ہم کہاں ہوتے، اگر حسن نہ ہوتا خود بیں؟

ہرزہ ہے، نغمۂ زیر و بمِ ہستی و عدم
لغو ہے، آئنۂ فرقِ جنون و تمکیں

لافِ دانش غلط و نفـــعِ عـبـادت معلوم
دردِ یک ساغرِ غفلت ہے، چہ دنیـا و چہ دیں

جلوہ پرداز ہو، نقشِ قدم اُس کا، جس جا
وہ کفِ خاك، ہے ناموسِ دو عالم کی امیں

نسبتِ نام سے اُس کی ہے یہ رتبہ کہ رہے
اَبداً، پشتِ فلك، خَم شدۂ نازِ زمیں

LITERAL TRANSLATION

The world is no more than a manifestation of the uniqueness of the Beloved;
But for the Beauty that seeks its own awareness, we ourselves would not exist.

Each place and instant sings, in varying measure, a song of being and non-being; it is fruitless.
Absurd and meaningless is the looking glass that mirrors the difference between insanity and self-possession.

The claims of knowledge are wrong and the gains of worship are unknown;
World and Faith are mere dregs in the cup of unknowing.

Wherever his footprint reveals itself,
That handful of dust is the trusty for the integrity of the two worlds.

Through the association of his name, this earth has gained such a central place in the order of creation
That the sky's back is forever bent to greet the earth.

These are, in the original couplets from a *qaseedāh* (a panegyric) addressed to Ali, the nephew of Mohammed, The Prophet of Islam. The structure of the *qaseedāh* requires the poet to begin with general considerations and only then come to specific praise.

FIRST COUPLET

Essential vocabulary:

Dehr: Temporal world. The word is used in Islamic theology to signify that which owes its span of life to the Eternal Will. Two basic concepts: that this sphere of creation is destructible; that its specific function is to reveal in material terms that which is beyond matter—pure, indestructible essence.

Jalvā: Indirect manifestation, in the sense of the Creator being manifest in what He creates; and Direct Revelation, as in the myth of Moses where God revealed Himself to Moses for a split instant. The later category of experience is, by definition, accessible only rarely and in brief encounters with the Infinite.

Māshooq: The Beloved. As in all metaphysical and speculative verse, God is conceived as The Supreme Beloved.

Khud-been: Literally, the word means "one who looks at himself." It signifies "one who seeks awareness of Self," or "Self seeking its Identity."

General explanation:

Metaphysical verse. God is perceived through three related Islamic concepts: God as Beloved; God as Creator; God as the ultimate principle of Beauty.

The original concept is this: just as man and his universe owe their existence to God, God too could not reveal Himself to Himself without creating the temporal world. Thus, the act of creation is God's necessity, the absolutely necessary act of self-realization. World is God reflecting upon himself.

SECOND COUPLET

Essential vocabulary:

Aiynā: looking glass, mirror. It is one of the oldest and most consistently employed images in Persian and Urdu traditions of poetry. It is an image of perfect truth. Also clarity. Man and time can leave their traces upon everything except the mirror. In the mirror, your absence is as clearly recorded as your presence. It is an impartial arbiter of truth.

Junoon: Madness. Not quite as despicable as in Western traditions. The word goes back to the given name of Majnoon (the man who was mad), the most famous of Arabia's ancient lovers. King Lear has never surprised readers of Urdu poetry: he is simply a man who gains knowledge through, and in, madness. Perfectly plausible.

Tamkeen: Self-possession, wisdom, ability to analyze.

Both are ways of reaching the same knowledge, and are equally good. The fact that one kind of knowledge is more readily available for analytic assimilation hardly matters.

THIRD COUPLET

Essential vocabulary:

Dānish: Whereas *Tamkeen* (translated in the previous couplet) is the act of knowing, *Dānish* is the faculty, as well as the possession, the sum, of knowledge.

Ghaflat: Literally, torpor. Something which is neither sleep nor wakefulness. Maybe, trance. It can certainly be induced by drugs (too great a preoccupation with the world or with the religious may act as the opiates which induce this state). The word is freely used in common speech to mean the state of trance in which one finds himself if running high temperature. Loss of consciousness, temporary or permanent. Sleep. Death.

Dunyā: World of verifiable objects.

Deen: Faith, religion. More specifically, belief in existence (of Man, God, objects). Ghalib often finds himself doubting the existence of the world with the best of all possible Platonic doubts: Does the world really exist: Or, is it merely the creation, or reflection, of my own senses? If the world is God's creation, which it is, we can't legitimately say that it really exists. Not *per se.* Not in itself. The terror of non-being is central to this concept of God.

FOURTH COUPLET

Essential vocabulary:

Jalvā-pardāz: *Jalva* has been described in the *Essential vocabulary* of the first couplet. This is a composite word. *Pardazi* means "to write," "to leave an imprint," "to adorn."

Nāmoos: Integrity, respect, purity.

Do-Ālam: Meaning two, or both, worlds. Again, two words used as one to signify the inseparable nature of the two worlds, of here and hereafter.

Ameen: One who is trusted with the duty, or responsibility, of looking after, safeguarding, property, safety, claims, etc.

FIFTH COUPLET

Essential vocabulary:

Rutbā: Place of honor, an office carrying great authority and dignity. A Secretary of State has a high *Rutbā* in the Administration.

Nāz-e-Zameeñ: *Zameeñ* is, simply, earth. *Naz* is conceit, elegance; authority, but not precisely that. It is an attitude gained not so much by being in authority as by being beautiful and, more certainly, by being loved. More than an attitude, it is an air assumed by those who are loved, know that they are loved, and that they can over-extend themselves without running the risk of losing their lover. I do not know a word in the English language which could adequately express this Urdu concept: I don't think the concept itself is strong or pervasive enough in Anglo-Saxon cultures for the language to yield and crystallize the meaning in a single word.

General explanation:

The underlying concept is conventional. It has an oblique relationship to a certain kind of Romantic pantheism: nature, earth, and elements being the true agents and exponents of the divine will. The central idea, at the heart of this pantheistic observation is, however, Islamic: that man, not the elements, is the truest, noblest of all creation; elements are there for man to harness them and they, therefore, pay homage to man.

It is in the light of this, the latter part of the concept, that the metaphor is understandable. The sky is the sphere of the elements: the earth is the sphere of man—therefore, the superior sphere: the sky pays homage to the earth. The metaphor, in a cosmic image of the sky bending like a dome and the horizons coming down to touch the sprawling earth, conceives of the two as a lover kneeling at the beloved's feet, her whim and will being his command.

It might be interesting to note that one of the names given to Ali was "Abu-Turab": "Father of the Earth."

Only Love has brought to us the world:
Beauty finds itself, and we are found.

All time, all places, call—here, not here:
no mirror finds the truth but in itself.

To know—what do we know? To worship—
emptiness takes us into its craving.

Any trace, glimpse, whatever flickers—
that's all we have, known or not known.

Held by the word, targeted here in openness,
Earth receives the sky bent forever in greeting.

William Stafford

There is only one beloved face
  but it is everywhere

    not seeing it we are nothing
    not revealed in its eyes

Each place at each moment sings
  of what is
  of what is not

    between madness and self-possession a senseless
    mirror dangles

Knowledge thinks it knows
  and piety in its blindness
  and the world and faith are left in the bottom of the cup
  of unknowing

Where you find the beloved's
  footprint
  the dust there is the seal of both worlds

And heaven bows down in love without end

    toward the earth

    Where the name is known
    to visit

            W. S. Merwin

GHAZAL

❊ II ❊

بسکہ دشوار ہے ہر کام کا آساں ہونا   آدمی کو بھی میسر نہیں انساں ہونا

وہی دیوانگی شوق! کہ ہر دم مجھ کو   آپ جانا اُدھر اور آپ ہی حیراں ہونا

جلوہ، از بسکہ، تقاضای نگہ کرتا ہے   جوہرِ آئنہ بھی چاہے ہے مژگاں ہونا

لے گئے خاك میں ہم داغِ تمنای نشاط   تو ہو اور آپ بصد رنگ گلستاں ہونا!

کی، مرے قتل کے بعد، اُس نے جفاسے توبہ   های اُس زود پشیماں کا پشیماں ہونا!

LITERAL TRANSLATION

(It is found that) it is difficult for every task to get easy;
Even man cannot attain to the condition of being Man.

What madness of attachment is it that I should every instant in that direction
Go by my own will/volition and all by myself become perturbed/astonished/
    amazed (at not finding her there).

Inasmuch as the appearance (of the beloved) demands that it be seen,
The substance of the mirror, too, wants to take the place of eyelashes.

We have taken with us into our grave the scar of the unfulfilled desire for
    happiness;
Now you are (here) and your embellishment of yourself with a hundred
    colors like/of a blooming orchard.

She vowed not to torment me only after killing me;
O, the recantation of this one who is quick to recant!

FIRST COUPLET

Essential vocabulary:

There are two words for "man" in Urdu, and the difference can't be really fully indicated merely by capitalizing the word "man" when translating the second word. It is extremely difficult to convey the difference; it is mainly a matter af how these words feel to the native speakers of Urdu. The word "Aadmi," obviously derived from the word "Adam," is the simple word, meaning "man" in the ordinary sense of the word. "Insān," although not as abstract as Man with a capital M, points to a certain sophistication, goodness, and that condition which distinguishes man from the mere animal level of existence; no suggestion of greater rationality or intellectual powers, only more humane, sympathetic, alive. ——

SECOND COUPLET

Essential vocabulary:

Shoq: Translated here as "attachment." Can also be translated as "yearning" or "predilection."

General explanation:

Verse about the natural condition of an impatient lover who expects his beloved even when she is not expected, or much before she is really expected.

THIRD COUPLET

Essential vocabulary:

Taqāzā: Coaxing, demanding, importuning.

Johar: Translated here as "substance." Genius, real essence, the true substance, nucleus.

General explanation:

Please refer to the explanation of the word "Saiqal" in the discussion of Ghazal V, couplet 4. The polishing of the mirror was done with extremely fine strokes, thinner than pencil shafts. This polish *is* the real substance of the mirror; each little stroke is so anxious to register the true beauty of the beloved's appearance that it wants to be like the lashes of the lover's eyes, expectant and open.

FIFTH COUPLET

Essential vocabulary:

Taubāh: Vow not to sin, commit crime, be unjust.
Pasheemān Honā: To be ashamed of what one is or has done.
Zood Pasheemān: One who is quick to recognize mistakes.

General explanation:

The second line is obviously ironical: what is the use of recanting now that all is over?

Nothing comes very easy to you, human creature—
least of all the skill to live humanely.

Time after time ahead of time, you fool,
standing in panic at the meeting-place.

The molecules of the mirror, if she appear,
longing to open like eyelids and take her in.

My body in the grave, scarred with its disappointments,
and yours, alive as the rainbow glistening through the orchard.

Killing me off she sobs: "I never meant to hurt you!"
Tears of repentance, wept three seconds too late.

Adrienne Rich

GHAZAL

❦ III ❦

سادگیہای تمنا، یعنی   پھر وہ 'نیرنگ نظر' یاد آیا

زندگی یوں بھی گزر ہی جانی   کیوں ترا راہگزر یاد آیا؟

پھر ترے کوچے کو جاتا ہے خیال   دلِ گم گشتہ، مگر، یاد آیا

کوئی ویرانی سی ویرانی ہے!   دشت کو دیکھ کے گھر یاد آیا

میں نے مجنوں پہ لڑکپن میں، اسد   سنگ اٹھایا تھا کہ سر یاد آیا'

LITERAL TRANSLATION

Simplicity of our desires! Meaning that
Again we remember her who cast a spell on our eyes.

Life could have passed anyway!
Why did we remember the way on which you tread.

Again, my thoughts go to your street!
But, I remember the heart (my heart) that has been lost (there).

What utter wilderness it is!
Seeing the desert, I remember my house.

In my boyhood (boyishness), Asad, I had once lifted a stone (to throw) at
   Majnooñ;
But, immediately, I remembered my own head.

Form:

Very short lines, of approximately three feet each.

FIRST COUPLET

Essential vocabulary:

Nairang-e-Nazar: "Nazar" means "sight"; hence, eyes. "Nairang" —bewitching artfulness, magic, miracle, a fascinating performance, which appears in many colors and guises. The phrase is used here for the beloved herself.

THIRD COUPLET

Essential vocabulary:

Koochā: Translated here as "street." Literally, that part of a neighborhood where one lives.

FOURTH COUPLET

Essential vocabulary:

Dasht: Translated here as "desert." Where nothing grows. More like barren or waste land.

Veerani: Translated here as "wilderness." Desolation. That eerie quality that abandoned houses have.

General explanation:

The effect is all in the sound of the first line: "Koi veerāni si veerāni hai!"

FIFTH COUPLET

Essential vocabulary:

Majnoon: A celebrated lover of ancient Arabia. Here named simply as great lover. His real name was "Qais." The word "Majnoon" literally means "insane" and was given to him as a second name.

General explanation:

In English, this verse sounds rather stupid and "corny." In the original, however, I find it one of Ghālib's most poignant verses.

There is, first, the question of cultural allusions. Majnoon was a lover so absorbed in his inner life that, for all his appearance, he looked insane and when he crossed streets children would throw stones at him, as is common among street urchins in Persian and, indeed, in Pakistani and Indian societies.

Then, there is verbal ambiguity. "Larakpan" means both "boyhood" and "boyishness." In one sense, it would mean "when I was a boy I wanted to do what all frivolous boys do"; in another sense, it would mean "out of my boyish ignorance I came close to desecrate what is sacred." Beyond these two meanings, however, there is an intricate allusion to the story of Majnoon. It is said that Majnoon fell in love with Laila, his beloved, when both were little children, barely at the end of elementary school. Thus, by mentioning boyhood and his own awareness, even at that young age, of the great lover that Majnoon was, Ghālib draws attention to the further implication that lovers recognize each other as of the same community and that he, too, had a premonition that he was going to be another great lover and that others would be stoning him just as they once stoned Majnoon. Considering the literal meaning of the word "Majnoon," the play on the word is obvious.

Old, simple cravings! Again
we recall one who bewitched us.

Life could have run on the same.
Why did we call her to mind?

Again, my thoughts haunt your street;
I remember losing my wits there.

Desolation's own neighborhood.
In the desert, my own house rises.

I too, like the other boys,
once picked up a stone to cast

at the crazy lover Majnoon;
some foreboding stayed my hand.

Adrienne Rich

GHAZAL

❧ IV ❧

جاتا ہوں داغِ حسرتِ ہستی لیے ہوے ، ہوں شمعِ کُشتہ، درخورِ محفل نہیں رہا

بَر روے شش جہت درِ آئینہ باز ہے یاں امتیازِ ناقص و کامل نہیں رہا

وا کر دیے میں شوق نے بندِ نقابِ حسن ، غیر از نگاہ، اب کوئی حائل نہیں رہا

دل سے ہوائے کِشتِ وفا مٹ گئی کہ واں ، حاصل، سوائے حسرتِ حاصل نہیں رہا

بیدادِ عشق سے نہیں ڈرتا، مگر، اسد جس دل پہ ناز تھا مجھے،وہ دل نہیں رہا ۲

LITERAL TRANSLATION

I go/depart, taking with me the scars of my unfulfilled desire to have lived
(better, longer, in a better condition or time);
I am (like) an extinguished candle, no more becoming/befitting in an
assembly of friends.

To the six appearances, the door of the mirror is opened;
Here, any distinction between the perfect and the defective is gone.

Ardor has undone the binding strings of the veil that concealed Beauty;
But for the sight itself, there is nothing in between.

From my heart, the desire to cultivate fidelity has disappeared/died because,
there/in that place,
There is nothing to be gained except the vain desire to gain (no reward, only
a vain expectation of reward).

I am not afraid of the cruelty of love, but Asad,
The heart that I was once proud of is no more (what it used to be).

FIRST COUPLET

Essential vocabulary:

Hasrat: Translated here as desire. Longing, to repine for, regret.

Hasti: Translated here as "to have lived." Existence, being.

Mehfil: Translated here as "assembly of friends." A get-together. Definite sense of rejoicing, light-heartedness.

SECOND COUPLET

Essential vocabulary:

Dar-e-Āynā: "Door of the mirror." In the metaphor, the mirror is conceived as something that you enter and go out of, a place where people may or may not be admitted. As has been pointed out earlier, the mirror plays a complex part in the traditional imagery of the Urdu ghazal. A mirror is that which reflects the true nature of things, a symbol of clarity and impartial judgment, therefore an image of disinterestedness on the one hand, and clarity of soul on the other.

General explanation:

Multiplicity of appearances has made clear perception impossible; such distinctions are now meaningless.

THIRD COUPLET

Essential vocabulary:

Shoq: Yearning, predilection for, ardor, zeal.

Band: Translated here as "the binding strings." Could well mean "button-hole." As a verb, the word means "to close."

General explanation:

Mystic verse. Beauty is a divine principle, it is not *seen*; it is revealed and then internalized through surrender. Great enough ardor will surely reveal it, but surrender implies surrender of senses, including that of sight. Beauty is conceived of its own concealment.

FOURTH COUPLET

Essential vocabulary:

Kisht: Literally, cultivation of a crop. Here, Ghālib is using the word in the sense of cultivating a habit, a view of life, a permanent pattern of conduct.

Vafā: Translated here as "fidelity." Keeping of a promise, being true in love, being good (to).

Miī Gayee: Translated here as "died," or "disappeared." Literally, is erased.

FIFTH COUPLET

Essential vocabulary:

Asad: Ghālib's first name, which he also used in his early Urdu poetry as a pen-name; he adopted the name "Ghālib" first for his Persian verse, then began using it for Urdu as well.

When I leave I'll hurt like a man beaten up
by his old gang, a man who got what he asked for.
Dropped like a used lightbulb, I won't be shocked.

There's no way to fix what's happened inside me.
Even with a door I probably shouldn't go back in.

For a time white heat drew me on to undress her, I
forget who. It was the spaces between us that I loved.

What can you get watching a life run like clockwork?
It is time to go when you don't even want loyalty.

Love could become more harsh, so what? Weather
changes that way. You see, I've nothing to be proud of.

William Hunt

I go now, wearing the scars of my hope for a better time;
I'm a pinched-out candle, no longer good for the banquet-table.

The door of the mirror no longer opens to the six senses;
here the distinction between defect and perfection is lost.

An ardent hand has undone the binding-strings of the veil,
but there is nothing behind it that sight can pierce.

I have given up cherishing faithfulness in my heart; because there
no reward exists, only the vain desire of reward.

I don't shrink at the cruelty of love; but, Asad,
the heart that I took pride in once is no longer what it was.

Adrienne Rich

No more campaigns. I have lost them all.
A doused light, I can't stand all the convivial fraud.

I can't find the truth. The world reflects
crooked, or the crystal ball distorts. The seer turns blind.

The brilliant and the real—I still know it's there,
but you never attain it by jiggling the senses.

So, it's dead in my breast, the zeal, the principle—
its only reward was the gleam while it vanished.

To you, my younger self: I still face the cruel game,
but this heart that beat hopeful can't take it any more.

William Stafford

GHAZAL

⚜ V ⚜

درد کا حد سے گزرنا، ہے دوا ہوجانا   عشرتِ قطرہ ہے، دریا میں فنا ہوجانا

باور آیا ہمیں پانی کا ہوا ہوجانا   ضعف سے، گریہ مُبدّل بدم سرد ہوا

روتے روتے غمِ فرقت میں، فنا ہوجانا   ہے مجھے، ابر بہاری کا برس کر کھلا

نہ چشم کو چاہیے ہر رنگ میں وا ہوجانا   بخشے ہے جلوۂ گل، ذوقِ تماشا، غالب

دیکھ برسات میں سبز آئنے کا ہوجانا   تا کہ تجھ پر کھلے اعجازِ ہوای صیقل

LITERAL TRANSLATION

The happiness of the drop is to die in the river;
When the pain exceeds bearable limits, the pain itself becomes the medicine.

Our weakness is such that tears have turned into mere sighing.
Now we really believe that water can turn into air.

When the spring cloud clears after heavy rain, it seems to me as if it were
Weeping so hard that, at the end it simply dies (from excess of grief).

So that you may begin to understand the miracle of the altering/polishing winds,
You should see how the mirror becomes green in spring.

The appearance of the rose has vouchsafed us the desire to witness (and enjoy), Ghālib!
Whatever the color and condition of things, the eyes should always be open.

FIRST COUPLET

Essential vocabulary:

Ishrat: Happiness, joy, ecstasy.

Fanā Honā: To die, to be consumed, to become so much a part of something that separateness is overcome.

General explanation:

The ultimate joy for the part is in once again being reconciled with the whole.

SECOND COUPLET

Essential vocabulary:

Dam-e-Sard: Translated here as "sighs." Literally, "cold breath"; that is how you say "sighing" in Urdu.

General explanation:

Weakness is so great that we can't even weep any more; can only sigh. That which was being shed in tears has now become cold breath; water has turned into air. Since we know that water can turn into air only in very high temperatures or in great heat, we can understand that suffering must be really great.

FOURTH COUPLET

Essential vocabulary:

Havāi-Saiqal: Translated here, very inadequately as "the polishing wind." Actually, it is far more complicated than that. "Saiqal" refers to the old way of making mirrors. It is the word for the particular kind of polish that was applied to the back of a mirror, as well as the process of applying this polish. "Hava-i-Saiqal" would thus mean the "winds of Saiqal." The point is that this polish was of a green color; thus, the back of the mirror is always

green. In the spring, however, the face of the mirror, too, turns
green (with mildew). Thus, it is proved that natural air can
change the color and function of things as much as artificial polish
does.

FIFTH COUPLET

General explanation:

The whole ghazal, it seems to me, is about the process of change.
The drop falls in the river and dies; this is the ultimate joy for it.
Water becomes air as the body grows weaker. Seasons change and,
with seasons, the colors too. And this, the final couplet is, in my
opinion, a celebration of change and acceptance of it as the eter-
nal, joyous process.

Waterbead ecstasy: dying in a stream;
Too strong a pain brings its own balm.

So weak now we weep sighs only;
Learn surely how water turns to air.

Spring cloud thinning after rain:
Dying into its own weeping.

Would you riddle the miracle of the wind's shaping?
Watch how a mirror greens in spring.

Rose, Ghalib, the rose changes give us our joy in seeing.
All colors and kinds, what is should and be open always.

Thomas Fitzsimmons

The drop dies in the river
of its joy
pain goes so far it cures itself

in the spring after the heavy rain the cloud
disappears
that was nothing but tears

in the spring the mirror turns green
holding a miracle
Change the shining wind

the rose led us to our eyes

let whatever is be open

W. S. Merwin

GHAZAL

❧ VI ❧

ستایشگر ہے زاہد اس قدر جس باغِ رضواں کا   وہ،اك گلدستہ ہے ہم بیخودوں کے طاقِ نسیاں کا

کیا آئینہ خانے کا وہ نقشا، تیرے جلوے نے   کرے جو، پرتوِ خرشید، عالم شبنمستاں کا

مری تعمیر میں مضمَر ہے، اك صورت خرابی کی   ہیولیٰ برقِ خرمن کا ہے، خونِ گرم دہقاں کا

خوشی میں نہاں، خوں گشتہ لاکھوں آرزوئیں ہیں   چراغِ مردہ ہوں، میں بیزباں، گورِ غریباں کا

نظر میں ہے ہماری، جادۂ راہِ فنا، غالب   کہ یہ شیرازہ ہے عالم کے اجزای پریشاں کا

LITERAL TRANSLATION

The garden of Rizwān (paradise), of which the zealot/recluse sings such praises,
Is a mere bouquet in the niche of forgetfulness for us who live in a state of oblivion and ecstasy.

In the hall of mirrors, your appearance has created the condition
Which the reflection of the sun would in a world of dewdrops.

Hidden in my constructions are ways of ruin(ing):
The warm blood of a farmer has in it the potential (of revolt) as there is potential electricity hidden in unthreshed corn.

Thousands of unfulfilled desires are hidden in (my) silence;
I am (like) an extinguished lamp on the speechless grave of a destitute.

Ghālib! the path of Death is always before our eyes;
For, this is the sum of this world's scattered elements.

Form:

Each line of approximately fourteen syllables.

FIRST COUPLET

Essential vocabulary:

Zāhid: Translated here as "zealot." Recluse, abstinent, devout, one who shuns the pleasures of this world.

Bāgh-e-Rizwān: "Bāgh" means garden. "Rizwān" is the keeper of paradise. Thus, the composite word means the garden of Rizwan," meaning "paradise."

Bai-Khud: Literally, one who is beside himself. Suggestion of drunkenness. Also piety: lost in the love of the divine. Not conventional piety, however.

Tāq-e-Nisyān: "Tāq" means a vault or recess in the wall. "Nisyān" is forgetfulness or oblivion. Despite its ambiguity, the metaphor suggests (1) a little vault where one may put something and then forget where one has put it; (2) an obscure corner to which one may retire if one is intoxicated, in a state of ecstasy or oblivion.

General explanation:

Rejection of conventional piety. One is religious not for the sake of the reward which the zealots say await the pious but because of the ecstasy which is available in religious experience here and now, ecstasy which is much greater than anything one may be promised.

SECOND COUPLET

Essential vocabulary:

Āynā-khānā: Translated here as "the hall of mirrors." In Ghālib's day, some aristocratic houses would have had mirror-work on the walls and the ceiling with thousands of little pieces of mirrors, each of which would naturally reflect the face of the person coming into the room.

Naqshā: Translated here as "condition." Literally, map.

Parto: Translated here as "reflection." Can also mean sunbeam or splendor.

Shabnamistān: "Shabnam" means "dew." The whole word would mean "world of dew."

General explanation:

The comparison between a thousand mirrors reflecting the entering beloved and a thousand dewdrops reflecting the sun, also between the splendor of the beloved and the sun, is quite obvious. There is, however, a more subtle, underlying meaning 'as well. Under the sunbeam the dew cannot last for too long, as if the splendor of the sun is too great for it to bear. Perhaps the mirror cannot bear the splendor of the beloved's reflection in the same way.

THIRD COUPLET

Essential vocabulary:

Kharābi: Translated here as "ruin(ing)." In fact, the word, unrelated to other words, would mean state of ruin, desolation, old age, valuelessness.

Soorat: Translated here as "ways." Literally, shape.

Hiula: Basic element of any matter, nucleus, potential, possibility.

Barq-e-khirman: Literally, electricity (or lightning) of unthreshed corn. Indicates the possibility that, if threshed too hard, the dry husk may give off sparks.

Dehqān: Literally, one who works on the land, hence, farmer or peasant.

General explanation:

Meaning depends on the metaphor. Unthreshed corn is spread on the ground and beaten so that the husk may be separated from the grain. But, if beaten too hard, the dry husk will produce sparks. Similarly, the farmer (1) lives close to the earth and (2) is close to the ground, owing to his poverty and the repression he lives under. He too, if repressed too much, may revolt and, in revolting, destroy what he himself makes. Similarly, like the husk and the farmer, the lover too, if made to go through too many hardships, may destroy the love which is as natural to him as grain to the husk and the production of crops to farmers.

It is a matter of interest to me that Ghālib would think of this metaphor. Peasant revolts are rather a rarity in subcontinental history. Only in Ghālib's time, when the British were consolidating their rule in Northern India, did the peasants revolt often enough for it to become a conceivable metaphor in poetry.

FOURTH COUPLET

Essential vocabulary:

Khun-gashtā: Translated here as "unfulfilled." Literally, covered with blood. Therefore, killed mercilessly and left unburied.

Āarzoo: Translated here as "desire." No true equivalent. It is a desire that remains, or is destined always to remain, unfulfilled.

Charāgh: Translated here, as it always is whenever Urdu or Persian poetry is translated into English, as a "lamp." It is a special kind of lamp—a round, open bowl of dried clay, with oil and convoluted cotton wick in it.

Murdā: Translated here as "extinguished." Literally, dead.

Bai-zubān: Literally, tongueless. Meaning, as translated here, "speechless." Specifically, being in such a bad, pitiable condition that one cannot even complain. The word is often used for infants and animals in distress.

Ghareeb: Translated here as "destitute." Poor. But also a man who is in an alien land, a stranger, a foreigner. A man generally in a bad way.

General explanation:

Meaning is, as often in Ghālib, in the metaphor. It is a common practice among the Pakistanis and among Indian Muslims to leave a well-lit lamp near the graves of their dead, at least while the grave is fresh. If a grave is fresh but the lamp is not lit, it only means that there is no one to tend the dead, i.e., he is either very poor or a stranger in the place, so that there is no one to care for him. It is interesting that Ghālib compares himself neither to the dead destitute, nor to the grave, but to the lamp which no one is there to light. No one to fulfill his wishes, therefore he is silent like the extinguished lamp. It is not so much a matter of self-pity, but that of a poignant and visually vivid image of desolation. To light a lamp is a mark of sanctity and a mark of respect. By removing the attention from death and the grave to the unlit lamp, Ghālib introduces an element of controlled grief and silent suffering.

FIFTH COUPLET
Essential vocabulary:

Nazar maiñ hai: Is in sight, before one's eyes, always under consideration, a part of all thinking.

Fanā: Phenomena of death, decay, inevitability of death, mortal nature of existence.

Sheerāzā: Translated here as "the sum." The word "sheeraza-bandi" means "stitching the back of a book," therefore putting together.

Even God's Paradise as chanted by fanatics
merely decorates the path for us connoisseurs of ecstasy.

Reflected among spangles, you flare into a room
like a sunburst evaporating a globe of dew.

Oh, buried in what I say are shapes for explosion:
I farm a deep revolt, sparks like little seeds.

Thousands of strangled urges lurk in my silence;
I am a votive lamp no one ever lighted.

Ghalib! Images of death piled up everywhere,
that's what the world fastens around us.

William Stafford

GHAZAL
❦ VII ❦

یہ نہ تھی ہماری قسمت کہ وصالِ یار ہوتا   اگر اور جیتے رہتے، یہی انتظار ہوتا

رے وعدے پر جیے ہم، تو یہ جان، جھوٹ جانا   کہ خوشی سے مر نہ جاتے، اگر اعتبار ہوتا

رگِ سنگ سے ٹپکتا وہ لہو کہ پھر نہ تھمتا   جسے غم سمجھ رہے ہو، یہ اگر شرار ہوتا

اسے کون دیکھ سکتا، کہ یگانہ ہے وہ یکتا   جو دوئی کی بو بھی ہوتی، تو کہیں دوچار ہوتا

یہ مسائلِ تصوف، یہ ترا بیان، غالب!   تجھے ہم ولی سمجھتے، جو نہ بادہ خوار ہوتا

LITERAL TRANSLATION

It was not our good fortune to meet our love.
However long we lived, we would still be waiting for such an encounter.

If we lived on your promise, then, you must understand, we did not believe it;
For, we would have died of happiness if we had believed your word.

From the vein in the stone would have flown such profusion of blood that it
would be unstoppable,
If what you think is grief were a spark of fire.

Who can/could see him/her, for he/she is unique, incomparable;
If there were even the faintest chance of duality/being possibly comparable to
someone else, we would have surely met him somewhere.

These matters of mysticism, Ghālib! And this exposition of them that you
give!
We would have thought you a mystic if you were not given to drinking so
much.

Form:

Each line of approximately fourteen short syllables.

FIRST COUPLET

Essential vocabulary:

Visāl: Literally, union or encounter. Neither word is really sufficient, since the original word conveys a sense of consummation neither of the English words suggests.

General explanation:

The first line should be read: If I tell you that I lived on your promise, you should not believe what I say. "We" is a mannerism to be avoided in English.

THIRD COUPLET

Essential vocabulary:

Rag-e-Sang: Literally, vein or sinew of the stone.

Gham: "Grief," suffering, torment.

General explanation:

The heart is being compared to stone. If grief was strong enough, it would have created a state of anguish comparable to the cutting of a stone.

FOURTH COUPLET

Essential vocabulary:

Yagānā, Yaktā: Unique, only one of its kind. Ghalib uses both words.

Dui: Extremely difficult to explain exactly. The condition of having someone else exactly like oneself, possibility of being duplicated, lending one's essence to another being.

Boo: Literally, smell. I have translated it here as "the faintest chance"; obviously incorrect in a literal sense.

General explanation:

1. Quranic concept of God: He is born of none, and none is born of him.

2. In Urdu pronouns have no gender. Genders are indicated by the verb; even there, it is possible to conceal them. Hence, him/her in the first line of the translation.

3. As can be seen quite easily, Ghālib has used the device of the conditional statement in all the four couplets we have translated here: if this, therefore that.

4. Once we grasp the religious connotations of this couplet, we are aware of the ambiguity of the first two couplets, particularly the second one which otherwise looks very silly, sentimental nonsense. Now, remembering that for the Muslim mystic death is a joyous journey toward God, we can read the second couplet thus: Had I believed in the notion that the soul is reconciled with God through death, I would have gladly died; but that is a promise in which I never believed, therefore chose to live! This, in turn, reinforces the ambiguity of the first couplet: It was not our good fortune to be reconciled to God while living (not reconciled to His Faith, but to Himself, finally), and we would have waited for this final reconciliation no matter how long we lived. Read together, the two couplets could finally mean that the soul's search for an encounter with God is perhaps ultimately in vain.

FIFTH COUPLET

General explanation:

Alcohol, which Ghālib consumed in vast quantities, is forbidden to Muslims. Anyone who drinks at all, let alone so immoderately, cannot claim to being even a Muslim in any orthodox sense. It is a verse of wholesome, tongue-in-cheek self-congratulation.

It wasn't my luck to achieve heavenly bliss.
No matter how long I lived, I'd never have made it.

Live on the great promise? Well, you can believe it;
I'd have died of joy had The Great One proved The Word!

This stone would have pulsed blood all over
if man's common suffering had really struck fire.

But who could ever find the True Mate, the Right One?
Could we sniff out soul-food, surely we'd do it.

These high, religious longings, Ghalib! These vaporings!
You'd seem religious if you didn't drink so much.

William Stafford

GHAZAL

❧ VIII ❧

بزمِ شاہنشاہ میں اشعار کا دفــتَر کُھلا   رکھیو، یارب، یہ درِ گنجینۂ گوہر کُھلا!

شب ہوئی، پھر انجمِ رخشندہ کا منظر کُھلا   اس تکلف سے کہ گویا بتکدے کا در کُھلا

گو نہ سمجھوں اُس کی باتیں، گو نپاؤں اُس کا بھید   پر یہ کیا کم ہے کہ مجھ سے وہ پری پیکر کُھلا

کیوں اندھیری ہے شبِ غم؟ ہے بلاؤں کا نُزول   آج اُدھر ہی کو رہے گا، دیدۂ اختَر، کُھلا

کیا ہوں غربت میں خوش، جب ہو حوادث کا یہ حال   نامہ لاتا ہے وطن سے نامہ بر اکثر کُھلا

LITERAL TRANSLATION

In the Emperor's banquet/court, a flow of poetry has begun.
Keep, O God, the door of this treasure of pearls open.

Night has come; again, the scene of beaming/glistening stars has opened,
With such profusion/extravagance as if the door of an idol-temple had opened.

Though I do not understand her talk/speech/conversation, though I do not understand her mystery/secret,
This alone is better than nothing that the fairy-faced one has begun to open up with me (has begun to talk to me).

Why is the night of grief so dark? Why afflictions/evil spirits are descending/alighting?
Will the open eyes of the stars remain turned to that other side?

How can I stay happy/contented while away from home when the nature of misfortunes is such that
The letter the messenger brings from home is often unsealed/open?

FIRST COUPLET

Essential vocabulary:

Bazm: Same as "Mahfil." Assembly, get-together, informal meeting.

SECOND COUPLET

Essential vocabulary:

Takalluf: Extravagant propriety, splendor in arrangement, profusion of good things. Can also mean "extreme formality," but that is not the meaning here.

But-kadā: Literally, house of icons or idols. The word is often used, in the stylized vocabulary of the ghazal, to signify the beloved's house, or a house where beautiful women live.

THIRD COUPLET

Essential vocabulary:

Pari-Paikar: With the face of a fairy, angelic, very beautiful.

FIFTH COUPLET

Essential vocabulary:

Ghurbat: We have discussed the word "Ghareeb" earlier. "Ghurbat," translated here as "while away from home," is the condition of being "Ghareeb." The condition of being destitute *and* away from home.

Havādis: Plural of Hādisā, accident. Events, unfortunate ones, beyond one's control, misfortunes one has to bear.

Vatan: Homeland, as well as the city or town from where one comes. Much stronger sense of belonging than "hometown" or an equivalent English term could possibly suggest.

General explanation:

For a mid-nineteenth-century man of the culture which Urdu represents, a sense of being at home and living in the privacy of a few friendships and affections is the highest value in day-to-day life. If one is away from home, there is no greater affliction than censored mail. Not so much a question of ideological eavesdropping, as that of intrusion in one's privacies. Ghālib would have had a great sense of anguish if he had lived in the modern society of bugged telephones.

We lean in the full moon as would a circle of gods
passing a window. Together our voices rise in song.

To those below, our lamp is mistaken for a star.
But the true stars lie at the bottom of the bowl.

Her voice spirals to me from the other side of moons.
Her expression tells me of secret springs, jewels, ice.

How long will I stand alone against broken walls?
Once I watched how a star fell behind her blue gown.

There is no message that will satisfy the mystery I sense.
Even secret letters from my home arrive here torn open.

William Hunt

Here in the splendid court the great verses flow:
may such treasure tumble open for us always.

Night has arrived; again the stars tumble forth,
a stream rich as wealth from a temple.

Ignorant as I am, foreign to the Beauty's mystery,
yet I could rejoice that the fair face begins to commune with me.

Why in this night do I find grief? Why the storm of remembered affliction?
Will the stars always avert their gaze? Choose others?

Exiled, how can I rejoice, forced here from home,
and even my letters torn open?

William Stafford

GHAZAL
❧ IX ❧

بندگی میں بھی وہ آزادہ و خودبیں ہیں کہ ہم   اُلٹے پھر آئے، در کعبہ اگر وا نہ ہوا

سب کو مقبول ہے دعویٰ تری یکتائی کا   روبرو کوئی بت آئنہ سیما نہ ہوا

سینے کا داغ ہے، وہ نالہ کہ لب تک نہ گیا   خاك کا رزق ہے، وہ قطرہ کہ دریا نہ ہوا

ہر بن مو سے، دم ذکر، نہ ٹپکے خوناب   حمزہ کا قصہ ہوا، عشق کا چرچا نہ ہوا

قطرے میں دجلہ دکھائی نہ دے،اور جزو میں کل   کھیل لڑکوں کا ہوا، دیدۂ بینا نہ ہوا

LITERAL TRANSLATION

Even in prayer, we are so independent/unfettered and self-examining that,
In case the door of the Ka'ba was not open, we would just come back
(instead of knocking and seeking admittance).

Every one accepts your claim for being unique;
No idol/icon, reflecting you as a mirror, can come face to face with you.

The complaint that does not reach the lips leaves a mark on the heart;
The drop of water that fails to become a river is simply the food for clay/
dust/earth.

If, at the time of telling, blood does not flow from each eyelash,
The story would not be of love but merely (as simple as) the story of Hamzā.

If it can not see the entire Tigris in a drop and the whole in a part,
Such an eye would merely be a child's game, not the eye of a wise man.

Form:

Each line of about twelve syllables.

FIRST COUPLET
Essential vocabulary:

Bandagi: Prayer, paying respects, dependency.

Khud-been: Translated here as "self-examining." As has been pointed out in the translation of Ghazal I, the word literally means "one who looks at oneself." Self seeking its own identity.

Kā'bā: The most sacred of Muslim shrines, a pilgrimage tò which is one of the essential duties of a Muslim.

SECOND COUPLET
Essential vocabulary:

But-e-Āynā-Seemā: Three words. "But" (pronounced like "put" with a soft "t") means "idol" or "icon." "Aynā" means "mirror." "Seemā" means "resembling." Hence, an icon that resembles the subject as a reflection in a mirror would resemble the person reflected.

General explanation:

Simple, clear assertion of the Islamic faith that God is incomparable essence and cannot be worshipped through idols.

THIRD COUPLET
Essential vocabulary:

Rizq: Literally, food. That which is consumed; that which nourishes.

General explanation:

How does a drop of water become the river? By being a part of it, by losing oneself in it. If you become a part of something you become that thing. Hence, the oneness of true lovers. Hence, the oneness, or possible oneness, of the soul and the divine that the souls seek. It is the nature of water, of drops, to seek the river, just as it is the nature of man to seek God, or, to say the same thing, the nature of the part to seek its whole.

As often happens in Ghālib, the associative content of the metaphor is even richer than the actual content of that for which the metaphor is first created.

FOURTH COUPLET

Essential vocabulary:

Hamzā: the hero of one of the most famous, voluminous, old tales of Urdu. A kind of picaresque, easy-going tale.

General explanation:

Meaning: A tale is not a tale of true love if it does not make the listeners cry and shed tears of blood. It is a minor verse, not of any great interest as a comment on, or celebration of, love. Implicit in the imagery, however, is a cultural setting which may be of interest.

The tradition of fiction in Urdu has until very recently, until Ghālib's own time that is, been very largely an oral tradition. Professional storytellers would tour towns and villages, people would congregate in community houses or the houses of some leading citizens, the storyteller would begin his tale well after dinner, and keep weaving longer and newer episodes partly from memory and partly with the aid of his own ingenuity until the early hours of the morning. The great crisis of art came toward the end of the night when the listeners would be tired and sleepy, and the story-teller would have to employ all possible resources of his art to keep their attention. If he did not win over sleep, his own and others', he wasn't much of a storyteller. The tale of Hamzā was one of the most famous and successful of these popular tales; it is to this day a classic of Urdu prose. What Ghālib seems to be saying here is that if the listeners were merely absorbed in the tale of Hāmza, instead of being emotionally and vividly involved in the story of love being told to them, the storyteller had obviously failed in his purpose and the duty of his art.

FIFTH COUPLET

Essential vocabulary:

Dajlā: Tigris. Euphrates and Tigris are the most often-mentioned rivers of the tradition of ghazal, like the Ganges of Hindi or the Brahmaputra in Bengali. Here, Ghālib does not particularly *mean* Tigris. Any river would serve the purpose. The question is of see- ing the whole river in the single drop which is a part of it.

Deedā-e-Beenā: Most interesting. Here I have translated it as "the eye of a wise man." Certainly means that, but also more: "The eye that can *see.*" "*Deedā*" means "the eye." "Bennā" would literally mean "he who can see." It also means *wise,* but only be- cause the wise man is the man who can see what others cannot.

General explanation:

This goes back to our discussion of the third couplet of this ghazal. The question of seeing the whole in the part, of part being the whole, of the part being nothing if it does not signify whole. And, it is for the seeing, the wise man to see the whole.

I have often thought of this couplet as a very good definition of the form of the ghazal, the whole business of poetry reaching for the essentials, rather than the details of experience, observation, etc.

A man in me sleeps. Even through my prayers,
he closes doors and calls out to be taken home.

No one denied you your memory of wings:
those clouds, although faces, are not your own.

I stay in, but cannot avoid the talk about love;
captured in the broken mirror, I find the rainstorm.

Only the sleepwalker embodies pure concentration.
Without division I would be at ease in this labyrinth.

My prayer of clouds. His dream of rain. I see a mirror
before which I awaken as a child that just died.

William Hunt

Even at prayer, we bow in our own image;
if God didn't hold His door open, we'd never enter.

He has no image: outside, everywhere, so distinctly
Himself that even a mirror could not reflect Him.

Held behind lips, lament burdens the heart; the drop
held to itself fails the river and is sucked into dust.

If you live aloof in the world's whole story,
the plot of your life drones on, a mere romance.

Either one enters the drift, part and whole as one,
or life's a mere game: Be, or be lost.

William Stafford

GHAZAL

❧ X ❧

کیوں جل گیا نہ، تابِ رخِ یار دیکھ کر؟   جلتا ہوں، اپنی طاقتِ دیدار دیکھ کر

آتش پرست کہتے ہیں اہلِ جہاں بھے   سر گرمِ نالہ ہای شرر بار دیکھ کر

ثابت ہوا ہے گردنِ مینا پہ خونِ خلق   لرزے ہے موج مَی، تری رفتار دیکھ کر

بک جاتے ہیں ہم آپ متاعِ سخن کے ساتھ   لیکن عِیارِ طبعِ خریدار دیکھ کر

گرنی تھی ہم پہ برقِ تجلّی، نہ طور پر   دیتے ہیں بادہ، ظرفِ قدح خوار دیکھ کر

LITERAL TRANSLATION

Why wasn't I burnt/consumed in fire, having seen the luster of the friend's face;
I burn, seeing my own powers of sight/my own ability to see, without losing sight, such splendor.

The people of the world call me a fire-worshipper,
Seeing me busy in complaints which shed sparks.

The blood of many has been proved on the neck of the decanter;
Seeing you walk, the wave of the wine trembles.

We get sold ourselves, along with the wealth of poetry;
But only after seeing/making sure of the true inclination of the nature of the buyer.

The Illuminating Lightning was to fall upon us, not on the Sinai;
(They) give the wine only after seeing the receptacle of the drinker. (Wine should be given only after seeing the goblet of the drinker.)

FIRST COUPLET

Essential vocabulary:

Jalnā: Literally, the word means "to burn," "to be burnt," "to be consumed by fire or heat." In the first line, the word is based in this basic, literal meaning. In the second line, however, it is used with a more obscure meaning of "burning with envy." The verbal play is, of course, based on the notion that he is envious of himself.

Yār: Friend, lover. Could mean, in this context, God.

General explanation:

Underlying the whole verse is the Muslim myth of Moses: God revealed Himself to Moses on Mount Sinai just for a flash (a flash of incomparable splendor), Moses was unconscious for a long while under the impact of the luster, and the mountain was burnt to coal and ashes.

THIRD COUPLET

Essential vocabulary:

Meenā: Decanter, goblet. One has to remember the shape of the Persian decanter to appreciate the visual image in the first line. A phrase is, in fact, used in Urdu to describe a slender and shapely neck, mark of great beauty, which would literally mean "neck having (resembling) a decanter."

Laraznā: To tremble, with fear, envy, etc.

General explanation:

Classic example of a poetic device in Urdu known as "Mahzoofāt," meaning "suppression" or "condensation"; in using this device, the poet would give the cause and effect, leaving the other links in the chain to the imagination of the reader. What Ghālib is, in effect, saying here is: people get attached to the bottle because (1) the neck of the decanter reminds them of yours, (2) the wine as it comes out of the decanter moves in shimmering waves, just as you move, and (3) the waves themselves tremble with envy, remembering the beauty of your walk and knowing that they will never move the way you move.

FIFTH COUPLET

Essential vocabulary:

Barq-e-Tajalli: "Barq" is "lightning," or one flash of lightning. "Tajalli" means luster, brightness, manifestation, illumination, appearance, beatific vision. Thus, the two words together would mean "the lightning luster of the beatific vision." However, as we have already said in the explanation of the myth of Moses, this flash burnt Sinai; the mountain could not bear such illumination.

Zarf: Translated here as "receptacle" or "goblet." This is perfectly correct. This meaning has, however, led to another: forebearance, power of tolerating, courage, etc.

General explanation:

I have given two alternative readings of the second line because the original syntax is kept intentionally ambiguous. Personally, I prefer the second reading: Wine should be given only after seeing the goblet/courage of the drinker. Particularly because that is really the only reading that explains the verse fully: The vision should have come to us, because we had the strength to bear its power, not to Mount Sinai, which lacked such strength.

Why didn't I shrink in the blaze of that face?
I flare up, apprehending the gaze that returned that vision unblinded.

Out in the world they call me a disciple of fire
because the words of my grief fall like a shower of sparks.

Many have fallen in love with the slim neck of the decanter;
seeing you walk, the wave of the wine trembles with envy.

We and the poems we make get bought and sold together;
but we knew all along for whom they were intended.

The lightning-stroke of the vision was meant for us, not for Sinai;
the wine should be poured for him who possesses the goblet.

Adrienne Rich

What we mistake for the ocean
I gave your name. The rest of my life
was spent building this ship.

My wife, my child, my father
walked further inland. Thin reeds,
they watched as I tore down our house.

Its frame sagged.
It begged for sails. Your body before me
swayed, filled with drowning.

What we are we choose to spend
in what we sing and I watch you
careless as those, who are without hope,
in love.

I have reached the thinnest horizon.
All of my words to you were for others
to share, but they are more
distant now than your arms.

William Hunt

GHAZAL
❧ XI ❧

لازم تھا کہ دیکھو مرا رستہ کوئی دن اور   تنہا گئے کیوں؟ اب رہو تنہا کوئی دن اور

جاتے ہوے کہتے ہو: قیامت کو ملیں گے،   کیا خوب! قیامت کا ہے گویا کوئی دن اور

تم ماہِ شبِ چاردھم تھے، مرے گھر کے   پھر کیوں نہ رہا گھر کا وہ نقشا کوئی دن اور؟

بجھ سے تمہیں نفرت سہی، نیّر سے لڑائی   بچوں کا بھی دیکھا نہ تماشا کوئی دن اور؟

ناداں ہو، جو کہتے ہو کہ کیوں جیتے ہیں غالب؟،   قسمت میں ہے مرنے کی تمنا کوئی دن اور ۱

LITERAL TRANSLATION

You should have waited for me a little longer.
Now that you have departed alone, you should stay alone a little longer.

On your way out you said that we shall meet next on the doomsday,
As if there was yet another day of doom.

You were, for my household, the moon of the fourteenth night;
Why did the affairs of my house not remain the same a little longer?

Agreed that you hated me and your relationship with Nayyar was strained,
You did not even stay a little longer to see your children play and grow.

Foolish are they who still wonder why Ghālib is still living;
It is his fate to stay alive, and wish for his death, a little longer.

Form: Approximately seven syllables to a line.

   This is an elegy for Ārif, the nephew of Ghālib's wife, who died
young and whose children Ghālib then adopted.

You should have waited for me a little longer.
Gone on alone, alone you should stay a little longer.

Leaving, you said we shall meet on Doomsday,
as if there could be another, any longer.

You were the full moon in the night for us.
Why couldn't we have stayed the same a little longer?

Yes, you hated me, and with Nayyar were unhappy,
but you didn't even watch your children play a little longer.

They are foolish who wonder why I am still living:
I am doomed to live, wanting death, a little longer.

William Stafford

GHAZAL
❧ XII ❦

نہ گُلِ نغمہ ہوں، نہ پردۂ ساز   میں ہوں اپنی شکستِ کی آواز

تو اور آرایشِ خمِ کاکل   میر اور اندیشہ ہای دور دراز

لافِ تمکیں، فریبِ سادہ دلی   ہم ہیں اور رازہای سینہ گداز

تو ہوا جلوہ گر، مبارک ہو   ریزشِ سجدۂ جبینِ نیاز!

مجھ کو پوچھا، تو کچھ غضب نہ ہوا   میں غریب اور تو غریب نواز

LITERAL TRANSLATION

(I) am neither the flower/ blossoming of song, not the curtain/ tapestry/
   web/shelter/note of music;
I am the sound of my own defeat/loss/breaking.

You are absorbed in the embellishment of your curls;
And for me are the concerns/apprehensions of matters far and long.

We brag of wisdom/foresight/self-possession, but it is merely the deception
   of a simple heart (creation of simple-mindedness);
We are occupied wholly with the secrets of an affable temper.

(Now that) you have appeared (have become manifest), be blessed
With the prostration/adoration of the forehead that bends (to touch the
   ground) for supplication/with longing.

(Now that) you ask for me, it is no wonder;
I am helpless/poor/afflicted/miserable, and you who look after the afflicted.

Form:

Approximately ten syllables to a line.

FIRST COUPLET

Essential vocabulary:

Gul-e-naghmā: Naghmā is "song." Gul, in Persian, means "the rose." In Urdu; it means "a flower." Here, it could mean "flowering."

Pardā-e-Sāz: Sāz (from Persian "Sākhtan"), literally, means "making"; also means a musical instrument, harmony or, more precisely, music. Pardā is a word with many meanings, including "veil" or "concealment." It could mean "a musical tone or mode," "a note of the gamut," or "note on a harp or a guitar."

Shikast: Normally, it means defeat. Here, it is used in its literal meaning: "breaking," "inner discord," etc. The word is also used for a note of music which does not agree or harmonize with the rest.

SECOND COUPLET

General explanation:

The poet sees the beloved arrange her hair, compares her curls with the snarls of his own thoughts, anxieties, etc., and also compares the length of her tresses with the lengths of the future he is concerned about. The hair is, like that of all beloved in Urdu poetry, presumably very black; therefore, the darkness of the hair and the darkness of his apprehensions, forebodings, etc.

THIRD COUPLET

Essential vocabulary:

Lāf: Boasting, bragging, claim.

Faraib: Deception, or self-delusion.

"Seenā" gudāz: "Seenā," literally means "breast" or "chest." "Gudāz" means "soft," "melted," "affable." Literal meaning— "that which can melt the breast"—would be ridiculous, though what it means to an Urdu reader is quite precise: a breast (where one bears one's misfortunes) made soft by grief.

General explanation:

The couplet is about the psychological fact that the people for whom love is an obsession would deceive themselves as well as others with the show of a foresight and self-possession which in fact isn't there, while they all the time are occupied with their grief and obsession. I think of Italo Svevo's *As a Man Grows Older* as an illustration of this kind of obsession.

FOURTH COUPLET
Essential vocabulary:

Sajdā: Prostration; Muslim form of worship. Does not necessarily make the verse religious; a kind of salute.

FIFTH COUPLET
General explanation:

Clearly religious in intent. Makes the preceding verse religious too.

I'm neither the loosening of song nor the close-drawn tent of music;
I'm the sound, simply, of my own breaking.

You were meant to sit in the shade of your rippling hair;
I was made to look further, into a blacker tangle.

All my self-possession is self-delusion;
what violent effort, to maintain this nonchalance!

Now that you've come, let me touch you in greeting
as the forehead of the beggar touches the ground.

No wonder you came looking for me, you
who care for the grieving, and I the sound of grief.

Adrienne Rich

Confession of a Happy Man

I have come to tell you
I am the music of my own defeat,
It is almost breaking
                        me.

How do you stay
And not seem to be destroyed
By these voices, these waters
          washing round you?

I am the sound of my own defeat,
Neither the flower nor the song blossoming.
I am neither the curtain nor anything
In the room.
I am not a made thing, not a shelter,
Not a note of music,
          surely I am not the tapestry
Nor anything fine.

You sit, so absorbed, so oblivious,
As if apprehension had left you long ago,
Made you like a silent sea that will never more
Endure a storm. You have created
Some new and original simple-mindedness,

Some ecstasy before which my longing must
Bow down. Even your curls are an invitation
To matters far and long. Your dreams? Yes
Now I see this,

You are set upon by dreams, pinned in
Their golden light, like Saint Sebastian
And his arrows. You sit like a fantastic
Roman saint caught in a wood that survives.
You sit dazed by dreams
      you've stolen from night.

Whether you have wisdom or merely appear to
Is something I worry about as I travel on.
So I remember your eyes and try to think
On their quality of round seeing.

These are the concerns of years now, of years.
And yet of wisdom you will tell me nothing.
Is it a path worth pursuing?
Is it the deception of a simple child?

When you smile I think we are wholly occupied
With the affable. I dream of going back
To worlds we've left, before I oppressed
The ocean, scarred the sky,
And made myself a pain to women. I look
Over your shoulders
And watch the stars burning, finding in
Them more friendliness, more loneliness.

David Ray

I am not a flower of song
        nor any of the bright shuttles of music
I am the sound of my own breaking

You think about how your hair looks
I think of the ends of things

We think we know our own minds
but our hearts are children

Now that you have appeared to me I bow
may you be blessed

You look after the wretched
no wonder you came
        looking for me

W. S. Merwin

GHAZAL
❧ XIII ❧

وہ فـــراق اور وہ وصال کہاں؟   وہ شب و روز و ماہ وسال کہاں؟

فرصتِ کاروبارِ شـــوق کیے؟   ذوقِ نظّارۂ جمـال کہاں؟

تھی وہ اک شخص کے تصور سے   اب وہ رعنائیِ خیـال کہاں؟

ایسا آساں نہیں لہو رونا   دل میں طاقت، جگر میں حال کہاں؟

مضمحـــل ہوگئے قُـــوا، غالبؔ   وہ عنـاصـــر میں اعتـــدال کہاں؟'

LITERAL TRANSLATION

Where are (no more) those meetings, those separations!
No more those days and nights, months and years!

Who has the leisure to indulge in matters of love!
No more is the delight of beholding the beautiful things!

It was from the imagination/vision of someone;
No more is the youth/grace of thought now!

Weeping (tears of) blood is not so easy;
No more is strength in the heart, stability in our condition!

Ghalib! my limbs are now feeble;
No more is any balance/ temperance/ equilibrium in the elements!

Form: Approximately seven syllables to a line.

All those meetings and partings!
Days, nights, months, years gone!

Falling in love takes time;
so enough of desiring and gazing.

It all took a certain force of vision
and the youth of the mind is over.

Shedding tears of blood is no game,
a strong heart, a steady nerve, are wanted.

I'm too old for an inner wildness, Ghalib,
when the violence of the world is all around me.

Adrienne Rich

No more those meetings, partings, tears!
No more those days, nights, months, and years!

Who has time for love, its lore?
Delight in beauty?—now no more.

All that was from the thought of someone,
a grace that's taken, now long gone.

Tears now hurt more; they flow deep.
Heartsick these days, it's blood we weep.

Oh, Ghalib!—weak limbs, no hope, disgust:
no balance now, even in this dust.

William Stafford

Gone are those meetings, those separations!
Those days and nights, months and years!

Who has time for dwelling on love!
Gone is the pleasure of looking at beautiful things!

It seems like a dream of another life.
Gone are those youthful turns of thought!

Gone are the tears of blood that used to come easy!
The heart is weak; the world cannot be trusted.

Ghalib! Your limbs have become feeble;
Gone is any justice in the scheme of things.

Mark Strand

GHAZAL

❈ XIV ❈

وگرنہ تاب و تواں، بال و پر میں خاک نہیں   مگر غبار ہوے پر، ہوا اُڑا لے جاے

کہ غیرِ جلوۂ گل، رہگزر میں خاک نہیں   یہ کس بہشت شمائل کی آمد آمد ہے؟

شرا بخانے کے دیوار و در میں خاک نہیں   خیالِ جلوۂ گل سے خراب ہیں مَے کش

سوای حسرتِ تعمیر، گھر میں خاک نہیں   ہوا ہوں، عشق کی غارنگری سے، شرمندہ

کُھلا کہ فائدہ عرضِ ہنر میں خاک نہیں   ہمارے شعر میں اب صرف دل لگی کے، اسد

LITERAL TRANSLATION

The wings are as dust (light, weightless, decomposed), so that the wind may perhaps take them away.
Otherwise, the feathers and the wings have neither strength nor forbearance.

What heaven-faced loveliness approaches (arrives) now
That the entire path has nothing, not even a speck of dust, save the illusion (appearance) of flowers.

Those who are intoxicated are so merely with the thought of the appearance of the flower:
Otherwise, there is nothing (nothing material, nothing that could cause their intoxication) in the walls, the door (and expanse) of the wine cellar.

I have been humiliated (thwarted, made humble, made to feel humble/ashamed, to feel small) by the destructive powers of (destructiveness, destruction caused by) my own love:
There is nothing in this house except the will to construct (more accurately, the wish to have constructed).

Now, Asad, my verses are mere pleasures of a pastime;
It is evident that nothing is to be gained by this display of talents.

Form:

Approximately fourteen syllables to each line. Slow beat, fairly heavily stressed.

FIRST COUPLET

Essential vocabulary:

Ghubār: Very thin, brittle dust, like sand, that goes easily in the wind. Dry, weightless.

Khāk nahiñ: Not even the dust, meaning "nothing," "is absent," etc. The phrase is used as a rhyme at the end of each couplet, and provides possibilities for all varieties of word-play.

General explanation:

The image of flight is a common image of strength in Urdu poetry, metaphors of birds like the falcon being used very often as symbols of energy, life, etc. Some such association is obviously in Ghālib's mind when he refers to himself here as a bird of flight.

The basic pathos of the metaphor is that the winds (alien elements) on which his wings used to soar are now so strong (too strong), and the wings so weak, so disintegrated, that instead of riding the wind, the wings are at the mercy of the wind.

It is to be noted that Ghālib does not use a personal pronoun. Are these his own wings, or those of his country?

SECOND COUPLET

Essential vocabulary:

Bahisht-Shimāyal: Bahisht (heaven, paradise); Shimāyal (like, having a similar aspect). It is to be noted that the likeness is not with an angel, but with the very heaven itself, not a specific being but a whole condition. Not the arrival of a person but a whole era.

General explanation:

The irony is so subtle, the vocabulary so rich in sound and sug-
gestiveness, that it took me years, literally years, to understand
that it *is* there. Since then, I have checked with a number of con-
temporaries, and all of them have confirmed my reactions. The
rhythm and the clarity of image create such a presence of "heaven-
faced beauty" arriving and of flowers sprouting to greet this
beauty, and there is such virtuosity in playing it against the
rhyme (Khāk Nahin—not a speck of dust), that the consequent
ambiguity is difficult to come to terms with even in the original.
However, the irony *is* there. I think Mr. Empson should read
these verses of Ghālib; he will have an idea or two. These are some
of the richest examples of ambiguity, provided they are read in the
original.

THIRD COUPLET

Essential vocabulary:

Khyāl-e-jalvā-e-gul: Composite of three words and two connecting
half-words: "Khyāl" (thought, imagination, wish), "e-" (of),
"jalvā" (appearance; the word has been fully discussed in explica-
tion of the first couplet of the first ghazal), "e-" (of), "gul"
(flower, specifically the rose, used here as a symbol of goodness,
beauty, peace, etc.).

Kharāb: Extremely common, but also extremely difficult word to
explain. Means bad, rotten, old, too old, or intoxicated. All the
varieties of meaning are implicit in the basic meaning: old. Re-
ferring to intoxicants, it would mean drunken, because old wine
is supposed to be quicker in these matters. However, the very fact
of being drunken also somehow signifies a condition of being
rather broken, or erôded.

General explanation:

An important clue for this couplet is the symbol of the rose, the thought that the rose *will* appear. We can understand the couplet to mean more or less this: there is nothing in the actual shape of events to promise any kind of resurgence; those who still hope have their faith in the impossible, and their hope is therefore itself a sign of how deeply disabled they are.

FOURTH COUPLET

Essential vocabulary:

Sharmiñdā: Literally, ashamed or regretting.

Hasrat: An unfulfilled desire to have done something, the consequent regret. Failure of accomplishment, and the regret of failure.

General explanation:

It seems to me that the subjective "I" of this verse is arbitrary unless the couplet is read in conjunction with the couplet that follows. Of course, the communal, or rather national, failure to effectively resist the British conquest is internalized in this image of personal failure. Yet, I have always felt that the house he is talking about in this couplet is not his own rather old, modestly furnished, much too dark and small house. Or maybe, the house in which he lived, which was filled with nothing but rats and borrowed books, was somehow associated in his mind with the city of Delhi which was crumbling like his own house, and with the surrounding, similarly falling, provinces of India.

FIFTH COUPLET

Essential vocabulary:

Arz-e-Hunar: Arz (humble expression, request), Hunar (genius, talent, skills).

General explanation:

Images of collective failure are now, in this couplet, finally, fully assimilated in an image of personal lack of worth and effectiveness, and of the irrelevance of the creative act itself.

Wings are like dust, weightless; the wind may steal them;
otherwise they would have neither power nor endurance.

What beauty now is bringing nearer the face of heaven
So that the path bears not dust but flower visions?

At the mere thought of the flower's face, some are drunk.
There is nothing else in the cellar, in the wineskins.

I have been shamed by my love's power to destroy.
In this house the wish to build lives alone.

Now Ghalib, these verses are idle amusements.
Clearly nothing is gained by such a performance.

W. S. Merwin

Now the wings that rode the wind are torn by the wind;
their feathers dust of the desert, their force shrivelled to powder.

What, who is this, coming our way, with the face of an angel,
that the dust of the bare road is lost in a carpet of flowers?

Anyone who still can hope is seeing visions.
The walls and doors of the tavern are blank with silence.

I am ashamed of the destroying genius of my love;
this crumbling house contains nothing but my wish to have been a builder.

Today, Asad, our poems are just the pastime of empty hours;
clearly, our virtuosity has brought us nowhere.

Adrienne Rich

GHAZAL
❦ XV ❦

سب کہاں، کچھ لالہ و گل میں نمایاں ہوگئیں ۔۔۔ خاک میں، کیا صورتیں ہونگی کہ، پنہاں ہوگئیں!

تھیں بَنَاتُ النّعشِ گردوں دن کو پردے میں نہاں ۔۔۔ شب کو ان کے جی میں کیا آئی کہ عُریاں ہوگئیں؟

نیند اُس کی ہے، دماغ اُس کا ہے، راتیں اُس کی ہیں ۔۔۔ تیری زلفیں جس کے بازو پر پریشاں ہوگئیں

ہم مُوَحّد ہیں، ہمارا کیش ہے تَرکِ رُسوم ۔۔۔ ملّتیں جب مٹ گئیں، اجزائے ایماں ہوگئیں

یوں ہی گر روتا رہا غالب، تو اے اہلِ جہاں ۔۔۔ دیکھنا ان بستیوں کو تم کہ ویراں ہوگئیں

LITERAL TRANSLATION

Not all, but only a few, are revealed in the rose and the tulip;
What faces those must have been that have gone (been hidden) under the dust!

The "daughters of the Bier" were, during the day, hidden behind a curtain (or, had hidden themselves behind the day's curtain);
What did they think (feel, occurred to them, came in their hearts) at night that they came out unconcealed (naked)?

To him comes sleep, belongs the mind (peace of mind), belong the nights
On whose arm you spread your hair.

We are the monotheists; breaking customs (traditions, set patterns) is our way of life;
Whenever the communities died, they became part of the faith.

If Ghālib continues to weep with this same prolixity, you, those who inhabit this world,
Will see that these cities shall become a mass of wilderness.

Form:

Each line of approximately fourteen feet. Fairly hard stresses.

FIRST COUPLET

General explanation:

Fairly simple verse about death. A kind of "Lo! the fair dead," or "Where are the snows of yesteryear," etc.

SECOND COUPLET

Essential vocabulary:

Banat-un-Nash: Daughters of the Bier; the three stars that go before the Bier are called "Banat."

Uryañ: Bare, naked, unconcealed.

General explanation:

A limited thematic continuation of the first couplet: human presence in the elements, etc., with obvious word-play on "daughters of the Bier." The Picasso-like imagery refers simultaneously to the pattern of stars that one can see on a clear night as well as the powerful sense of the unreal, of presences beyond the human and beyond the light of day, that pervade really still nights, the kind of reverent fear Wordsworth expresses in the best passages of *The Prelude.*

THIRD COUPLET

General explanation:

Hardly any difficulty, except perhaps observing the pleasure Ghālib takes in complimenting the lady on her hair.

FOURTH COUPLET

Essential vocabulary:

Millat: Community, nation, group.

Eemān: Faith. Less accurately, religion, belief. The concept is integral to Islam; the only concept of knowledge.

General explanation:

In Western concepts, or for that matter any ideology outside the communist, nation is that which unites. Not so in Islam. There, the effort is always away from Nationalism, always toward a totalization. At least in the harder core of Islamic thought, nationalism is that which sets you apart, apart from other nations. Thus the death that Ghālib is talking about is not so much a death as the assimilation of the communal identity within a larger, progressively total human reality. Again, "Eemān" is also to be understood in this Islamic, or Marxist-Sartrean, sense of progressively total knowledge. Totalization of the community is inseparable from totalization of knowledge in a very Hegelian sense. It is in this context that Ghālib's ideas of monotheism, community, and faith are to be understood.

Here and there in a rose or a tulip
      a few of the faces
      only a few

         but think of those that the dust
         keeps to itself

All day three stars
      the Daughters of the Bier
      hid in back of the light

         how was it for them when the night came
         and they stepped forth naked

Sleep comes to him
      peace belongs to him
      the night is his

         over whose arm your hair is spread

We make new
      our life is
      an overthrowing

         the great faith gathers to itself
         deaths
         even of its worshippers

W. S. Merwin

Almost none
of the beautiful faces
come back to be glimpsed for an instant in some flower

once the dust owns them

The three Daughters of the Bier
as becomes stars
hide in the light till day has gone

then they step forth naked
but their minds are the black night

He is the lord of sleep
lord of peace
lord of night

on whose arm your hair is lying

W. S. Merwin

Not all, only a few, return as the rose or the tulip;
What faces there must be still veiled by the dust!

The three stars, three Daughters, stayed veiled and secret by day;
what word did the darkness speak to bring them forth in their nakedness?

Sleep is his, and peace of mind, and the nights belong to him
across whose arms you spread the veils of your hair.

We are the forerunners; breaking the pattern is our way of life.
Whenever the races blurred they entered the stream of reality.

If Ghalib must go on shedding these tears, you who inhabit the world
will see these cities blotted into the wilderness.

Adrienne Rich

Only the survivors come forth in the rose, the tulip.
What faces have gone down under the dust!

All the star children curtained in the day—
how their hearts flooded, naked in the night!

Sleep comes, peace, quiet of rest,
for one who holds an arm under your hair.

We poets break through custom, find our way to life;
old ways die, and weave themselves into faith.

If the poet mourns this well, you dwellers in the world,
you will find your cities drifting back into the wild.

William Stafford

GHAZAL
❧ XVI ❧

کسی کو دیکھے دل، کوئی نواسنجِ فغاں کیوں ہو؟

نہو جب دل ہی سینے میں، تو پھر مُنہ میں زباں کیوں ہو؟

وہ اپنی خو نہ چھوڑیں گے، ہم اپنی وضع کیوں چھوڑیں؟

سُبک سر بن کے کیا پوچھیں کہ 'ہم سے سرگراں کیوں ہو'،

کِیا غمخوار نے رُسوا، لگے آگ اس مُحبت کو!

نہ لاوے تاب جو غم کی، وہ مـــیرا راز داں کیوں ہو؟

قفس میں مجھ سے رودادِ چمن کہتے نہ ڈر، ہمـــدم

گری ہے جس پـــہ کل بجـلی، وہ میرا آشیاں کیوں ہو؟

بہ فتنہ، آدمی کی خانـــہ ویرانی کو کیا کم ہے؟

ہوے تم دوست جس کے، دشمن اُس کا آسماں کیوں ہو؟

LITERAL TRANSLATION

Why should one, having given his heart to someone else, utter cries of pain?
If there is no heart in the breast, why should there be a tongue in the mouth?

She/he will not give up her/his habit; why should we change our way?
Why be humble and ask why she/he is angry?

The one with whom we shared our grief has made us infamous; may this love
be destroyed.
Why should one, who cannot bear my grief, be my confidante?

(Now that I am) in the cage, O friend! Don't fear telling me the story of the orchard.

The nest which was struck (and destroyed) by lightning yesterday —why must it necessarily be mine?

This trial is not insufficient to destroy one's house; If you were to be somebody's friend, he doesn't need the heavens to be his enemy.

FIRST COUPLET

Essential vocabulary:

Navā-Sanj-e-Fughān: "Navā" means a "loud cry." "Sanj" is put at the end of a word to mean "doing" or "having." Thus, "Navā-Sanj" means "one who utters loud cries" (for any purpose whatever). "Fughān" means "cries of pain."

SECOND COUPLET

Essential vocabulary:

Subak-sar: Translated here as "humble"; that is perfectly correct. Literally, however, it would mean "a person with a light head." Meaning, of course, humble.

Sar-garān: Translated here as angry; this, too, is perfectly correct. Literally, however, it would mean "person with a heavy head." Meaning, "angry." Thus, the two words are played against each other.

THIRD COUPLET

Essential vocabulary:

The phrase which has been translated as "may this love be destroyed" would, if literally translated, mean "may this love catch fire."

FOURTH COUPLET

Essential vocabulary:

Roodād: Translated here as "story." The story of that which has happened.

Hamdam: Translated here, correctly, as friend. Literally, "one who breathes in unison."

General explanation:

In the traditional imagery of the Urdu ghazal, the lover is the bird which goes to the orchard, or the garden, to look for his beloved, the flower (the bird is, invariably, the nightingale). There, in the garden, he may be caught and put in a cage. While thus in captivity, his nest may be destroyed by forces that be (natural forces, circumstances, cruelty or indifference of the beloved). The language is, of course, symbolic; the nest would, thus, be the basis of existence.

FIFTH COUPLET

Essential vocabulary:

Fitnā: Trial, torment, affliction, calamity.

Khānā-veerāni: Destruction of the place where one lives.

Dost: Friend. As has been pointed out earlier, it is common in Urdu to refer to the lover as friend.

Āasmāñ: Literally, sky; translated here, correctly I think, as "heavens."

Handing over my heart, where does this sobbing come from?
If the breast is emptied, can the mouth still have a tongue?

He'll never mend his ways; then why should I?
Why should I offer meekness for his violence?

I'd like to crumple this love, this shame into the fire;
what is this need to share what can't be shared?

Now I'm behind bars, go ahead, tell me the story—
that nest the lightning shriveled last night—why do you think it was
        mine?

What I'm living through now could smash my house in pieces:
my friend, with you on earth I don't need enemies in the clouds.

Adrienne Rich

GHAZAL
❧ XVII ❧

نیرے دل میں گر نہ تھا آشوبِ غم کا حوصلہ   تو نے پھر کیوں کی تھی میری غمگساری؟ ہائے!

شرمِ رسوائی سے جا چھپنا نقابِ خاک میں   ختم ہے الفت کی، تجھ پر، پردہ داری، ہائے!

خاک میں ناموسِ پیمانِ محبت مل گئی   اٹھ گئی دنیا سے راہ و رسمِ یاری، ہائے!

گوش مہجورِ پیام و چشم محرومِ جمال   ایک دل، تس پر یہ نا اُمیدواری، ہائے!

عشق نے پکڑانہ تھا، غالب، ابھی وحشت کا رنگ   رہ گیا، تھا دل میں جو کچھ ذوقِ خواری، ہائے!

LITERAL TRANSLATION

If your heart did not have the courage to bear the ennui raised by grief,
Why did you, alas (attempt to) share my sorrow.

O, to go and hide behind the veil of dust from the shame of infamy/ill reputation!
Alas, the secretiveness of love reaches its limit with you.

The dignity/honor of the promises of love have gone under the dust;
Alas! the ways (the tradition) of love/friendship is over in this world.

The ear is excluded from message and the eye is denied that vision.
A heart is left, but that too, alas, is drenched in such sorrow!

Ghālib! love had not yet taken on the color of madness (mad passion);
Whatever desire there was in our heart to be infamous (ill reputed, known as weak or wretched) is, alas, still, there, unfulfilled.

Form: Approximately twelve syllables in each line.

If you were frail of heart
why did you want to share my suffering?

Never was love so furtive as yours
hidden under a veil of dust.

Which buries the proud vows of love
and they leave no children.

No word reaches the ear, no vision the eye,
but the heart—its sorrow finds it.

Still, Ghalib, this love lacks the color of madness.
The heart courted disgrace, but there too it failed.

W. S. Merwin

GHAZAL
❧ XVIII ❦

آ، کہ مری جان کو قرار نہیں ہے　　　　طاقتِ بیدادِ انتظار نہیں ہے

دیتے ہیں جنت، حیاتِ دہر کے بدلے　　　　نشہ، باندازۂ خمار نہیں ہے

گریہ نکالے ہے تری بزم سے مجھ کو　　　　ہائے! کہ رونے پہ اختیار نہیں ہے

دل سے اُٹھا لطفِ جلوہ ہای معانی　　　　غیرِ گل، آئینۂ بہار، نہیں ہے

تو نے قسم میکشی کی کھائی ہے، غالب؟　　　　تیری قسم کا کچھ اعتبار نہیں ہے

LITERAL TRANSLATION

Come now; my spirit has no rest/peace (without you);
I have no strength (to bear) the cruelty of waiting (any longer).

They give/offer us paradise in exchange for life in this world;
The intoxication is not proportionate with the after-effects.

My own tears are forcing me out of your banquet;
Alas! I have no control over my own weeping.

The joys of the visions of meaning have left my heart;
Except for the blossoms, there is no mirror for the spring.

Ghālib! You have sworn not ever to drink;
But, there is no certainty in your oath (no certainty that you will keep it)

Form:

Approximately nine syllables to each line.

SECOND COUPLET

General explanation:

The meaning of the second line is: the reward is not commensurate with the act: there is such great joy in living that paradise shall be a disappointment after this, as a hangover after the joys of drinking.

FOURTH COUPLET

General explanation:

A sense of powerlessness, impotence. The heart no more registers the meaning of what is happening. The heart is in its period of decay, in its season of autumn. The only regeneration in the spring is in the flowers it brings; except for the flowers, there is no spring. Similarly, the evidence of the heart's strengths is in what it comprehends; if it brings no meaning, it may as well not be there.

Another reading of the couplet is:

Without the flowers, there is no spring; without the heart, there is no meaning.

Come now: I want you: my only peace.
I've passed the age of fencing and teasing.

This life: a night of drinking and poetry.
Paradise: a long hangover.

Tears sting my eyes; I'm leaving
lest the other guests see my weakness.

I is another, the rose no rose this year;
without a meaning to perceive, what is perception?

Ghalib: no hangover will cure a man like you
knowing as you do the aftertaste of all sweetness.

Adrienne Rich

GHAZAL

❧ XIX ❧

مری رفتار سے، بھاگے ہے بیاباں مجھ سے   ہر قدم، دوریِ منزل ہے نمایاں مجھ سے

صورتِ دود، رہا سایہ گریزاں مجھ سے   وحشتِ آتشِ دل سے، شبِ تنہائی میں

صورتِ رشتۂ گوہر، ہے چراغاں مجھ سے   اثرِ آبلہ سے، جادۂ صحرائی جنوں

آئنہ داری یک دیدۂ حیراں، مجھ سے   گردشِ ساغرِ صد جلوۂ رنگیں، تجھ سے

ہے چراغاں،خس و خاشاکِ گلستاں، مجھ سے ۱   نگہِ گرم سے اک آگ ٹپکتی ہے، اسد

LITERAL TRANSLATION

On every step, the distance of the goal from me is evident;
At my own speed, the desert runs from me.

In my night of loneliness, owing to the ferocity/grief of the fire in my heart,
The shadow eluded me like a waft of smoke.

Because of the blisters, the way in the desert of my madness
Remained illuminated like a chain of pearls.

From/Because of you is the motion of the colorful goblet that appears in a
  hundred ways;
Because of me is the mirroring (of the vision) in a single, astonished eye.

From my burning eye, a fire oozes out, Asad!
From/by/because of me is illuminated the soil and the dried leaves in the
  garden.

Form:

Approximately thirteen syllables to a line.

FIRST COUPLET

General explanation:

Image is of a man running through a desert. The faster he runs, the vaster the desert seems to be; the frontiers of the desert seem to be farther and farther away.

THIRD COUPLET

General explanation:

Visual image. If a man who has bleeding blisters on the soles of his feet walks through a desert, he will leave behind him a trail of bloodstains on the sand.

Where I'm going is farther at every step
the desert runs from me
with my own feet

In the lonely night because of the anguish
of the fire in my heart
the shadow slipped from me like smoke

The trail of my madness crosses the desert
red pearls on a page of manuscript

The goblet moves through all its colors because of you
the vision is caught in a single incredulous eye
because of me

And the eye bleeds fire
and the earth and dried leaves of the garden
are lit up because of me

W. S. Merwin

Every step I take unrolls the distance further;
racing the desert, it lengthens underfoot.

Through the bonfire my grief lit in that darkness
the shadow went past me like a wisp of smoke.

Footprints of blood in the path I traveled
lit up the desert, a track of crimson pearls.

You hand the cup around with a hundred supple gestures;
I hold it in the mirror of one astonished glance.

Fire licks out from the rims of my eye, Asad;
when I look at a dry leaf it starts to smoulder.

Adrienne Rich

With every step I took, my goal seemed farther away.
I ran my fastest, but the desert ran faster.

That lonely night fire inhabited my heart
And my shadow drifted from me in a thin cloud of smoke.

Because my feet were blistered in the desert
Of my madness, my wake shone like a chain of pearls.

Because of you the goblet had a thousand faces;
Because of me it was mirrored in a single eye.

Fire runs from my burning eyes, Asad!
I light up the soil and the dead leaves in the garden.

Mark Strand

GHAZAL

❧ XX ❧

کس کا سراغِ جلوہ ہے، حیرت کو، اے خدا؟   آئینـــــہ، فــرشِ شش جہت انتظار ہے

ہے ذرہ ذرہ، تنگیِ جا سے، غبارِ شوق   گر دام یہ ہے، وسعتِ صحرا شکار ہے

چھڑکے ہے شبنم، آئنۂ برگِ گل پہ، آب   اے عندلیب، وقتِ وداعِ بہار ہے

بے پردہ سوے وادیِ مجنوں گزر نکر   ہر ذرے کے نقاب میں، دل بیقرار ہے

اے عندلیب، یک کفِ خس بہرِ آشیاں   طوفانِ آمد آمدِ فصلِ بہار ہے

LITERAL TRANSLATION

Whose appearance is it, O God, the signs of which my amazement/astonishment/consternation has seen?
The mirror has become a six-tiered ground of waiting.

Owing to the scarcity of space, each little mote/particle/speck of dust has become a whole mist of longing;
If this be the net/cage, it is the breadth of the desert itself that has become the prey.

The dew scatters water now on the mirror of the flower-branch;
O nightingale, this is the time for the departure of spring.

Do not go unveiled toward the valley of Majnoon (the mythic lover)
Hidden behind the veil of each speck/atom of dust there is an impatient heart.

O nightingale! (give me) a fistful of sticks for the nest;
There is the storm of the first arrival of the season of spring.

Form:

Approximately twelve syllables to a line.

SECOND COUPLET

General explanation:

This world is small and full of people; each person is longing for the vision (which may or may not be vouchsaved). If the world was created to keep this illusion, the world itself has fallen prey to the illusion.

THIRD COUPLET

General explanation:

The phrase "Aab Dainā" has two meanings: "to give water," and to "polish a mirror." Hence, the metaphor of "water on the mirror of the flower-branch."

It is toward the end of the spring that dew is strongest in the subcontinent; when nights are too dewey to sleep outdoors, one knows that the spring is now about to end. The dew is shedding tears for the departure of the spring. The reference is also to an ancient Persian custom in which water was sprinkled on mirrors when someone had to go on a journey, with the belief that it would keep him safer from evils.

FIFTH COUPLET

General explanation:

In his life, spring is so brief that he has to build a nest with the first arrival of spring so that he may be safe after this brief spell is gone. Even spring comes like a storm.

Is it you, O God, whose coming begins to amaze me?
The mirror has turned to a six-tiered ground of waiting.

Every crowded speck of dust has become a whole mist of longing;
if this world is a net, the entire desert is its prey.

The dew has polished the sheen of the flowering branch.
The nights of spring are finished, nightingale.

Don't go unveiled into that valley of Majnoon:
every grain of sand there is an atom of desire.

Nightingale, give me a bundle of sticks for building:
I hear the thunder of the first days of our spring.

Adrienne Rich

GHAZAL

❦ XXI ❧

شبنم، بگلِ لالہ، نــہ خـالی زِ ادا ہے   داغِ دلِ بیدرد، نظـرگاہِ حیا ہے

قری، کفِ خاکسـتر و بلبل، قفسِ رنگ   اے نـالہ، نشانِ جگـرِ سوختہ کیا ہے؟

شعلے سے نہوتی، موسِ شعلــہ نے جو کی ٥ جی، کس قدر افسردگی دل پہ جلا ہے!

مجبوری و دعوایِ گرفتاریِ الفت   دستِ تـہ سنگ آمـدہ، بیانِ وفا ہے

اے پرتوِ خُرشیدِ جہاتـاب، ادھر بھی   سایے کی طرح، ہم بہ عجب وقت پڑا ہے

LITERAL TRANSLATION

The dewdrop on the red poppy is not without end/function/meaning:
The spot on the heart of her who is cruel is a place where shame has come (to pass).

The dove is merely a handful of ashes and the nightingale a prison of color;
O my cry, the scar of burnt heart is nothing (in comparison).

The fire itself could not have accomplished what the lust for fire has;
The heart has suffered much for fading of the spirits.

To claim to be love's prisoner is itself a consequence of constraint (compulsion):
The hand that comes under a stone (the weight of a stone) becomes a promise of eternal faithfulness (being eternally faithful).

O World-illuminating Sun! Cast your splendor here (on us, in this direction) too;
A strange time, like a shadow, has come upon us.

Form:

Each line of approximately 14 syllables.

FIRST COUPLET

Essential vocabulary:

Lālā: Red poppy, or tulip. The Indian poppy is smaller than the Western variety and, with the poetic license which is common in Urdu, one could imply that a dewdrop is sufficient to cover the black that lies at the heart of the flower. Matters are further complicated by the fact that, in the highly stylized language of nineteenth-century Urdu poetry, it is used as a metaphor for the heart, or for the eye. If the heart, it is a bleeding heart, like Shelley's. If the eye, always that of a woman who has been crying (eyes are therefore red). Thus, dewdrop on a red poppy could be tears in the bloodshot eyes of a woman.

Dāgh: Spot, speck, stain, stigma, scar, blemish, a mark burnt in.

Bai-dard: "Bai-" is simply a negative prefix, meaning "without." "Dard" is a word of peculiar complexity, in fact delicacy. It is pain, but it is also, more profoundly, sympathy. A person who is without "Dard" is not simply a man who can act painlessly, he is in a profound sense cruel, a man without essential sympathies. The concept has nothing to do with Victorian heartaches. This is in essence a concept produced by a society where friendship, as a human relation, is at least as important as love, and both relations are ultimately inter-related. Acting without love still leaves room for acting with sympathy, which is in itself equally important.

General explanation:

It is a verse about love, but with extreme metaphorical complexity. The first line is a pure metaphor, the second a simple statement. The second line is to be understood first. Acting cruelly, without sympathies, not only hurts the other person, it also leaves a scar, a blemish, a stigma on the heart of the person thus acting; this scar is something to be ashamed of. In the second line, we get a complex metaphor first to explain the same, then to extend the meaning. The poppy is the heart, the function of the dew is to hide the blemish. However, dew is again a metaphor for tears. Where do these tears come from? We come to the other metaphorical meaning of the poppy: the eyes. The meaning of the metaphor becomes clear. If the poppy is also the eye, and the dew is tears, then these are the tears the eyes shed in order to make up for, to wash away, to undo the blemish of cruelty. Thus, the function of the dew is not only to hide the blemish, but also to make up for it: regaining, or becoming capable of, sympathies even after the denial of love. Of course, denial of love is never explicitly mentioned; it is implicit in the whole action of the verse.

SECOND COUPLET

Essential vocabulary:

Qumri: Turtledove, ringdove.

Qafas-e-Rang: Precisely that, a prison of color. Not prisoner. It is somewhat unusual to come across a line which stresses the color, rather than the sound, of the nightingale.

Nālā: A cry of anguish. Complaint, lament.

General explanation:

In terms of sound, both the dove and the nightingale serve implicitly as metaphors for the poet's cry, or lament; both are singing birds. Visually, they both serve, particularly the dove, as images of the burnt heart.

THIRD COUPLET

Essential vocabulary:

Sholā: Literally, flame.

Havas: Lust, avarice, intense longing, base passion.

Jee: There is no single English equivalent for this simple col-
loquial expression meaning heart, spirits, even courage.

Afsurdagee: Melancholy. The condition of being withered, faded,
benumbed, depressed, dejected.

Dil: Literally, heart. In the original, Ghālib is playing on the
meanings of the words "jee" and "dil."

General explanation:

There is a great deal of word-play involved in the original. Be-
sides playing the word "jee" against "dil," Ghālib is also playing
on the expression "jee Jalnā." Literally, this expression means
"burning of the heart," implying suffering. Thus, to say that "the
heart burns because the heart has withered" and to play it against
the first line where he talks about the fire failing and the lust for
fire succeeding, produces strange verbal play; it becomes difficult
to follow the main argument of the lines. What is being said is,
however, comparatively simple. If we take fire to symbolize union,
preferably sexual, of the lovers, the meaning is easily accessible:
the union itself could not have been as apocalyptic as the failure
to meet; the sexual encounter itself might have killed the passion,
but to kill it through denial has involved greater suffering.

FOURTH COUPLET

Essential vocabulary:

Majboori: Constraint, necessity, being under compulsion.

Paimān: Promise, undertaking.

Vafā: Truthfulness, being faithful, keeping one's word.

General explanation:

True to his favorite method, Ghālib gives the correlative image in
one line and explains it in the other. Here, of course, the main

argument is stated first; explication through metaphor follows in the second line.

If a stone is too heavy to be lifted and one's hand is already pressed under the weight of that stone, there is nothing to be done but to stay with one's burden. (Camus's interpretation of the Sisyphus myth: Sisyphus loves his rock. The rock becomes, here as in Camus, the symbol for life, and love.)

Man is "condemned" to love, in the same sense as Malraux says man is condemned to live.

FIFTH COUPLET

Essential vocabulary:

Parto: Light, beam, splendor.

Jehān-tāb: That which illuminates, lends warmth to the world.

Dewdrop on poppy petal
there for a reason

in that place the cruelty of her heart can be
        concealed only by one of her own tears

The heart is burnt out
but its sufferings were nothing to yours
      oh my cry

          charred dove
          nightingale still burning

Worse than any fire fed by what was
was the fire of longing for what was not
        nothing was left of the spirit
        but the heart's suffering

Love holds him
prisoner he says
and something has him
      sealed

        like a great rock on his hand

Sun who turn everything into day
shine here too

a strange time
has come upon us like a shadow

                              W. S. Merwin

There's meaning in the teardrop that blurs the red eye of the poppy:
the heart that knows its flaw understands the need for concealment.

The turtle-dove is a heap of cinders, the nightingale a vivid cage of sounds;
O my cry, you are nothing to these.

The fire itself was no hotter than the lust for fire;
the spirit goes on trembling in the dead ash of its wanting.

The price love pays is part of love's necessity.
The hand unable to lift the stone is condemned to keeping faith.

Sun of the World! shed your illumination on us here;
a strange time, like a shadow, has fallen on us.

Adrienne Rich

Dew on a flower—tears, or something:
hidden spots mark the heart of a cruel woman.

The dove is a clutch of ashes, nightingale a clench of color:
a cry in a scarred, burnt heart, to that, is nothing.

Fire doesn't do it; lust for fire does it.
The heart hurts for the spirit's fading.

To cry like Love's prisoner is forced by Love's prison:
hand under a stone, pinned there, faithful.

Sun that bathes our world! Hold us all here!
This time's great shadow estranges us all.

William Stafford

GHAZAL

❧ XXII ❧

ہر رنگ میں بہار کا اثبات چاہیے   ہے رنگِ لالہ و گل و نسریں، جدا جدا

تقریب کچھ تو بہرِ ملاقات چاہیے   سیکھے ہیں، مہ رخوں کے لیے ہم، مصوری

اک گونہ بیخودی مجھے دن رات چاہیے   ئی سے غرض نشاط ہے، کس روسیاہ کو؟

رو، سوے قبلہ وقت مناجات چاہیے   سر، پاے خم پہ چاہیے ہنگامِ بیخودی

عارف، ہمیشہ مست ئی ذات چاہیے   یعنی، بحسبِ گردشِ پیمانۂ صفات

LITERAL TRANSLATION

The colors of the tulip and the eglantine are different;
(But) in every color, we should affirm (assent to) the spring.

We learn the art of painting/drawing for the sake of the moon-faced ones
   (beautiful women);
We need some pretext for the meeting.

What infamous man drinks (the wine) for pleasure;
I need a measure of forgetfulness day and night.

The head should be bent on the base of the wine-jar in the hour of forget-
   fulness;
The face should be in the right direction (towards the kaa-ba) at the time of
   prayer.

Meaning that (reference to the earlier couplet) according to the rotation of
   the goblet of properties/attribute/qualities,
The-one-who-knows should always be drunk on the wine of self-hood.

Form:

Approximately twelve syllables to each line.

SECOND COUPLET

General explanation:

Painting is a euphemism; Ghālib clearly means poetry, his own. In a segregated society like that of the Muslims, men have traditionally found it difficult to meet women. Not so the poets. As practitioners of highly respected art, they have had better opportunity. As a result, their sexual life has presumably been happier than that of the less fortunate ones whom the Muse does not visit.

THIRD COUPLET

Essential vocabulary:

Roo-siāh: Literally, one whose face is blackened. Meaning disgraced, unfortunate, infamous.

Bai-khudee: Literally, unaware of self. Meaning, forgetfulness.

FOURTH COUPLET

General explanation:

The ethic of a fullness of life; you combine the life of the spirit with the life of the passions, sacred and the profane.

FIFTH COUPLET

Essential vocabulary:

Aa'rif: The one who knows, sagacious, possessing knowledge of God, his ways, and of how to deal with them, the man to whom things have been revealed.

Zaa't: Self, essence or radical constituent of self.

General explanation:

Continues with the imagery of the last two couplets (wine, goblet etc.) and the meaning of the last one couplet. As the time changes, one should adapt oneself to the new occasion, according to one's own possibilities, not the callings of the convention.

Tulip or primrose, they have to speak in their colors.
Everyone answers the spring in his own dialect.

Poetry is really just a way of meeting poets;
and if they're good-looking women, so much the better.

What kind of man gets stoned for fun?
Day, night, I need obliteration for my grief.

Facing the bottle, the blotted mind knows what it's facing;
Facing the shrine the mind at prayer knows just as well.

The wine of the occasion changes its vintage,
but the great drinkers are always drunk on themselves.

Adrienne Rich

GHAZAL
❧ XXIII ❧

عشق مجھ کو نہیں، وحشت ہی سہی   میری وحشت، تری شہرت ہی سہی

قطع کیجے نہ تعلق ہم سے   کچھ نہیں ہے، تو عداوت ہی سہی

عمر، ہر چند کہ ہے برق خرام   دل کے خوں کرنے کی فرصت ہی سہی

ہم بھی تسلیم کی خو ڈالیں گے   بے نیازی، تری عادت ہی سہی

یار سے چھیڑ چلی جائے، اسدؔ   گر نہیں وصل، تو حسرت ہی سہی

LITERAL TRANSLATION

(I accept) what I have is not love but madness;
Let my madness be a source of reputation (notoriety?) for you.

Do not sever all relationships with us;
If nothing else, let there be enmity.

Although life passes fast as lightning,
Let it be an interval only for the heart's suffering.

We shall also make obeisance our habit;
Haughtiness/inattention/disregard may be your way.

Asad! Let an amorous skirmishing/incitement continue with her.
If not the meeting itself, let the desire for it suffice.

Form: Approximately nine syllables to a line.

Alright it's not love it's madness
you'll be known for it too

Let's not break off everything
even hatred

Life is a lightning flash
pain and all

May she still want to even if she can't

it might be enough

W. S. Merwin

Let's stop for relief
you take a trip, or I will,
find some dull landscape
Why look upon a body
that sets you atremble
makes you a fool with open mouth

Almost in love
        I think so
now that we have burned
        and eaten forty nights
broken windows with whispers

David Ray

I suppose my love for you is a form of madness.
Why shouldn't that madness play like fire about your name?

Don't let a nullity fall between us:
if nothing else, we could become good haters.

Our time of awareness is a lightning-flash,
a blinding interval in which to know and suffer.

My method shall be acquiescence and a humble heart:
you method may be simply to ignore me.

Don't lose heart in this skirmish of love, Asad:
though you never meet, you can always dream of the meeting.

Adrienne Rich

GHAZAL
❧ XXIV ❧

دیکھنا قسمت کہ آپ اپنے پہ رشک آجائے ہے

میں اُسے دیکھوں، بھلا کب یہ مجھ سے دیکھا جائے ہے؟

ہاتھ دھو دل سے، یہی گرمی گر اندیشے میں ہے

آبگینہ، تندیٔ صہبا سے پگھلا جائے ہے

غیر کو، یارب، وہ کیونکر منعِ گستاخی کرے؟

گر حیا بھی اُس کو آنی ہے، تو شرما جائے ہے

شوق کو یہ لت کہ ہر دم نالہ کھینچے جائیے

دل کی وہ حالت، کہ دم لینے سے گھبرا جائے ہے

سایہ میرا، مجھ سے، مثلِ دود، بھاگے ہے، اسد

پاس مجھ آتش بجاں کے کس سے ٹھہرا جائے ہے؟

LITERAL TRANSLATION

Look at my luck, that I envy myself.
That I should see her? How can I ever? (how can I bear to?)

If our apprehensions have such intensity of heat, we should abandon (give
up hopes of saving) the heart that suffers:
The glass goblet is about to melt because of the heat of the wine.

How can she, O Lord, forbid others from insolence/audacious conduct!
She shies away even if the insolence makes her ashamed.

My ardor now has the propensity to keep complaining every instant;
The heart is in such condition that it gets bewildered/flustered/
   anxious if I stop even for breath/relief.

Asad! My shadow runs from me like smoke.
My soul is on fire; who can stay near me.

Form:

Approximately fourteen syllables to a line.

FIRST COUPLET

General explanation:

The beloved (God or woman) has such splendor that even to be
able to look at her dazzles the eye, and needs such strength that
one envies oneself for having that strength.

General explanation:

The second line illuminates the first, by creating a correlative
metaphor.

THIRD COUPLET

General explanation:

This, and the next, couplet depend on verbal play; here, on the
word shame (in Urdu there are two different words: haya, mean-
ing shyness or to be abashed; and, sharm, meaning shame). Shying
away from a strong display of disapproval because of the sense of
shame as well as the natural shy disposition.

FOURTH COUPLET

General explanation:

The verbal play is on the word "dam": meaning "instant" (as in the first line), or "to breathe" as well as "stop for relief" (as in the second). The ardor has grown so much that he cannot help talking of his love all the time; even if he stops for breath, the heart gets bewildered and flustered.

FIFTH COUPLET

General explanation:

Shadow is in the man as smoke is in fire. When the fire rages, the smoke rises and leaves it. The smoke is never static, without motion; it is always getting away, always leaving, getting lost. Grief and loneliness are so great that even the shadow, the one inseparable part of man, will not stay with him.

I have had enough of flying.
It is the dust in the streets now
I'd like to descend to.

David Ray

I am so lucky I envy myself.
How is it that I am the one chosen to see her?

If I should weaken, I'd burn myself out.
Right now the wine's heat is beginning to melt the glass.

How can she, O Lord, forbid the bad manners of others!
She is shy to begin with and anger just drives her to shame.

My passion keeps me complaining, and I cannot stop.
If I caught my breath, I'd lose heart.

Asad! My shadow pours out of me like smoke.
My soul is on fire; nothing is mine for long.

Mark Strand

GHAZAL
❧ XXV ❧

کبھی نیکی بھی، اُس کے جی میں، گر آجاۓ ہے مجھ سے

جفائیں کرکے اپنی یاد، شرماجاۓ ہے مجھ سے

وہ بدخو، اور میری داستانِ عشق طولانی

عبارت مختصر، قاصد بھی گھبراجاۓ ہے مجھ سے

اُدھر وہ بدگمانی ہے، اِدھر یہ ناتوانی ہے

نہ پوچھا جاۓ ہے اُس سے، نہ بولا جاۓ ہے مجھ سے

سنبھلنے دے مجھے، اے ناامیدی، کیا قیامت ہے !

کہ دامانِ خیالِ یار چھوٹا جاۓ ہے مجھ سے

قیامت ہے کہ ہوۓ مدعی کا ہمسفر، غالب

وہ کافر، جو خدا کو بھی نہ سونپا جاۓ ہے مجھ سے

LITERAL TRANSLATION

If it ever comes to her mind to be good toward me,
She remembers her cruelties of the past, and shies away.

She is short-tempered and my tale of love long!
I should be brief; even the messenger gets bored with me.

On that side there is such mistrust, on this side such weakness!
Neither can she ask, nor am I able to speak.

Let me pull myself together, O despair! what calamity is this?
I am beginning to lose even the thread of thought about my love.

Formalities aside! Even though it is only when she reveals herself,
That she should be seen is a thought unbearable for me.

Form:

Approximately fifteen syllables to a line.

FIFTH COUPLET

Essential vocabulary:

Takalluf Bartaraf: Formalities aside. Meaning: "without mincing words, or matters."

General explanation:

The verse is possibly religious. Even if God reveals Himself, the thought of seeing Him with the naked eye is unbearable for the devout.

If ever it occurs to her to be kind to me
        she remembers how cruel she's been
        and it frightens her off

Her temper's as short as my tale of love is long
        much too long
        bores even the messenger

        and I despair
        and lose the thread of my own thoughts

        and can't bear to think of someone else
        setting eyes on her

                        W. S. Merwin

It flickers in her mind to be good to me:
past cruelties come; the mind shies away.

She is jealous, abrupt; and my love is long telling.
I can't be deft enough; our messenger gets bored.

Mistrust over there; weakness here:
she can't ask; I can't speak.

Let me try harder—despair! What goes wrong?
I lose even the drift of such difficult thought.

But get it straight: she reveals enough for me to know this:
I want something that is too good to be revealed.

William Stafford

GHAZAL
❧ XXVI ❧

مدت ہوئی ہے، یار کو مہماں کیسے ہوے   جوشِ قدح سے بزم چراغاں کیسے ہوے

پھر، گرمِ نالہ ہای شرربار ہے نَفَس   مدت ہوئی ہے، سیر چراغاں کیسے ہوے

ہمدگر ہوے ہیں دل و دیدہ، پھر، رقیب   نظّارہ و خیال کا ساماں کیسے ہوے

مانگے ہے، پھر، کسی کو لب بام پر، ہوس   زلفِ سیاہ رخ پہ پریشاں کیسے ہوے

جی ڈھونڈھتا ہے پھر وہی فرصت، کہ رات دن   بیٹھے رہیں تصورِ جاناں کیسے ہوے

LITERAL TRANSLATION

It is long since my Love was my guest,
Long since the bubbling goblet has illuminated our evenings together.

Again my breath comes hot with complaints that shed sparks (not words);
It is long since we have gone to visit (see) the illuminations.

The heart and the eye, though each other's enemies otherwise, are in unison again
In desiring the opportunities for seeing (the beloved) and imagining (pleasures).

Again, my longings for her to appear on her balcony,
Her black hair blown across her face.

Again, the heart seeks days and nights of leisure, as (were available) in the past,
So that I may spend my hours thinking of nothing and none other than my beloved.

Form:

Strongly stressed line of approximately seven syllables each.

FIRST COUPLET

Essential vocabulary:

Josh: Enthusiasm, brimming with life, bubbling when applied to wine-cup.

Qadah: Cup, goblet, wine-glass.

Bazm: Meeting of friends or intimates, a gathering of friends, in other words an intimate party.

SECOND COUPLET

Essential vocabulary:

Nālā-hāi: plural for Nālā, or complaint.

Sharar: sparks. Bar: shedding, or throwing.

FIFTH COUPLET

Essential vocabulary:

Fursat: Leisure, time free of worries and work, time to be alone.

It is a long time since my love stayed with me here
And the sparkling goblet lit up our evening together.

Again my complaining breath comes hot, showering sparks.
It is a long time since we saw the night filled with flares.

Again the old enemies, heart and eye, come together
Pining for chances to see her, to brood upon her.

Again I long for her to appear on her balcony,
the wind veiling her face in her black hair.

Again the heart yearns for free days and nights, as before,
to think of nothing and no one but her.

W. S. Merwin

It's been a long time, love,
since we sat talking and drinking.

My breath is hot again, I'm wordless;
shedding sparks is all I'm good for.

Sight and feeling, those old foes
are friends again, fused in desiring.

Again I watch for her at her window,
waiting for wind in her black hair.

I need to ward off visitors, letters,
hoarding my solitude for her.

Adrienne Rich

GHAZAL

❦ XXVII ❦

جتنے زیادہ ہوگئے، اُتنے ہی کم ہوے   بے اعتدالیوں سے، سُبک سب میں ہم ہوے

اُڑنے نہ پاے تھے کہ گرفتار ہم ہوے   پنہاں تھا، دام، سخت قریب آشیاں کے

وہ لوگ رفتہ رفتہ سراپا الم ہوے   مت پوچھ کہ ان عشق کی، پوچھے ہے کیا، خبر؟

ہر چند اس میں ہاتھ ہمارے قلم ہوے   لکھتے رہے جنوں کی حکایات خونچکاں

سائل ہوے، تو عاشقِ اہلِ کرم ہوے   چھوڑی، اسد، نہ ہم نے گدائی میں دل لگی

LITERAL TRANSLATION

Because of our intemperances, we have lost our worth among/for others;
The more we became (the more intemperate we became, the more we extended ourselves), the less (in worth, trustworthiness, respectability) we became.

A snare was hidden/laid very close to the nest;
We had not even had a chance to fly (away), when we were taken prisoner.

Do not ask for the news of those who bore the trials of love;
As the time passed (by and by, gradually), they have themselves become embodiments of grief.

We kept writing the blood-drenched narratives of that madness
Although our hands were amputated in the process.

Asad! We did not forego our original inclination (or, our sense of fun) even in begging for charity;
When we decided to become mendicants, we also became the lovers of the benign and the compassionate.

Form:

Approximately twelve syllables to a line.

FOURTH COUPLET

General explanation:

A highly sophisticated verbal pun here, in the phrase "hāth-qalam honā." The phrase means "amputation of hands," but the word "qalam" (used here as the verb "to amputate"), if used singly and as a noun, means pen. Thus, if read incorrectly or by someone who does not know the meaning of the verb "qalam honā" and reads it merely as a noun, the whole phrase could mean "our hands become pens."

FIFTH COUPLET

Essential vocabulary:

Dil-Lagi: has two alternate meanings—
1. Sense of fun, good humor, to joke.
2. To give one's heart, to apply one's attention, to persevere.

Ahl-e-Karam: "compassionate," "benign."

General explanation:

Two alternate readings of the couplet are possible, depending on how we read the word *dil-Lagi*. If we accept *dil-Lagi* to mean "sense of fun, or humor," we shall also have to accept that the word *Ahl-e-Karam* is used satirically. Then the couplet would mean: even in becoming a mendicant, I did not give up my sense of humor (rather a black, inverted kind of humor) and followed only those who pretended to be compassionate, thus making my career of mendicity deliberately as unsuccessful as the earlier career as a lover. As I had previously chosen cruel beloveds, now I chose uncharitable patrons.

Outrageousness has given me a bad name in the world;
Self-aggrandized, I've lost my honor among men.

There was a snare laid early, close to the nest;
Before we were in flight, it dragged us into the cage.

Don't ask for the old lovers, how they are doing:
little by little they've turned to facsimiles of grief.

We went on writing the histories of that madness
till our fingers dripped blood, and the hand became a pen.

Asad, even as beggars we were bent on failure,
our patrons gave us nothing besides compassionate smiles.

Adrienne Rich

GHAZAL
❧ XXVIII ❧

اے تازہ واردانِ بساطِ ہوای دل   قف زنہار! اگر تمہیں ہوس نای و نُوش ہے

دیکھو مجھے، جو دیدۂ عبرت نگاہ ہو   میری سنو، جو گوشِ نصیحت نیوش ہے

ساقی، بجلوہ، دشمنِ ایمان و آگہی   مطرب، بنغمہ، رہزنِ تمکین و ہوش ہے

یا شب کو دیکھتے تھے کہ ہر گوشۂ بساط   دامانِ باغبان و کفِ گلفروش ہے

لطفِ خرامِ ساقی و ذوقِ صدای چنگ   بہ جنتِ نگاہ، وہ فردوسِ گوش ہے

یا صبحدم جو دیکھتے آکر، تو بزم میں   نہ وہ سرور و سُور، نہ جوش و خروش ہے

داغِ فراقِ صحبتِ شب کی جلی ہوئی   اک شمع رہ گئی ہے، سو وہ بھی خموش ہے

LITERAL TRANSLATION

Desiring is like being on a dice- or a chessboard and you, who have newly
  arrived upon it,
If you are lusting to eat and drink (away your lives).

Look at me if you have eyes capable of learning an admonitory lesson,
Listen to me if you possess an ear able to listen to good advice:

The cupbearer, in her beauty, is an enemy of faith and reason
The singer, through songs, robs one of one's good sense and self-possession.

On the one side, at night we used to see that each corner of the carpet
Is like the lap of a gardener or the palm of a florist (both holding flowers);

The joy of seeing the cupbearer walk, the pleasure of hearing the harp:
This (one) is paradise for the eye, that (the other) is heaven for the ear.

On the other hand, if you come in the morning and look at the place
 where friends met,
You will find neither that drunken pleasure nor that ardor and
 effervescence,

Burnt-out in the grief for the breaking-up of the previous night's
 joyous meeting,
 A candle remains, but that too is silent and without flame.

Form: Approximately thirteen syllables to a line.

No explanation necessary.

You sensual novices, you are caught on a shuffleboard;
you stagger and pour away your lives.

Look at me, if your eyes can bring you a lesson;
listen to me, if your ears can take advice:

The barmaid looks ravishing—she blots faith and reason;
the singer, she steals away your senses.

All around us, at night, we used to yearn for
those random bundles of flowers, all around us—

Liquid walk of the barmaid, the zither's twang:
heaven for the eye, heaven for the ear.

But in the cold morning, abandoned by revelers—
no heaven, none of that old ardor.

A candle, ravaged for the carousing,
has guttered out; it too is silent, without any flame.

William Stafford

GHAZAL

❧ XXIX ❧

وہ بادۂ شبانہ کی سرمستیاں کہاں!   اٹھیے بس اب، کہ لذتِ خوابِ سحر گئی

اُڑتی پھرے ہے، خاک مری، کوے یار میں   بارے اب، اے ہوا، ہوسِ بال و پر گئی

دیکھو تو، دلفریبیِ اندازِ نقشِ پا   موجِ خرامِ یار بھی کیا گل کتر گئی!

ہر بوالہوس نے حسن پرستی شعار کی   اب آبروے شیوۂ اہلِ نظر گئی

نظارے نے بھی کام کیا واں نقاب کا   مستی سے ہر نگہ ترے رخ پر بکھر گئی

LITERAL TRANSLATION

Where are (no more are) the transports/ecstasies of drunken nights;
Awake/Arise, now! the joy of sleeping/dreaming in the mornings is gone.

My dust (the dust that I have become) is infamous now in my beloved's street;
But, O wind, there is now no desire for flying.

Look at the beauty (that entices/captures the heart) of the/her graceful footprints!
The wave of the beloved's walking has strewn wonderful flowers (where she has walked).

Every lustful man has taken the worship of beauty as his way (deceitful way);
Now, the honor of the ways/customs of those who had true sight is gone.

Seeing (itself) proved to be/acted as a veil there (on the face);
Because of the rapture/ecstasy, even my sight simply scattered around your profile.

Form:

Approximately twelve syllables to a line.

FIRST COUPLET

Essential vocabulary:

Bādā-e-Shabānā: Bādā (wine), Shabānā (of the night); therefore, "wine of the night." Nights of drunkenness, drunk nights. May even be a colorful euphemism for sleep itself.

Lazzat-e-khāb-e-Saher: Lazzat (great joy, pleasure), khāb (dream, ·sleep), Saher (morning). Thus, literally: joy of dream of morning. Meaning the luxury of sleeping late.

General explanation:

Luxury of ease is over; perhaps youth too. Nostalgia for better times in the past. Delhi has become a difficult city to live in, or to live with any joy.

SECOND COUPLET

Essential vocabulary:

Urti Phirai Hai: Is flying, hovering, around. Here, is infamous.

Havas-e-bāl-o-par: Havas (lust, intense desire), bal-o-par (feathers); therefore, desire for feathers. Translated here as "desire to fly."

General explanation:

The couplet is based on the familiar metaphor of Urdu love poetry: the lover as the bird (nightingale) that sings songs to the rose (the beloved). The lover is so weak now (presumably, shrunk in size too) that he is light as dust. The dust is flying around in the beloved's street, but the bird itself is no more; it has no feathers, and has no desire to regain them. Resignation.

FOURTH COUPLET

Essential vocabulary:

Bu-ul-Havas: Literally in Arabic one who fathers lust. Means "lustful man."

Ahl-e-Nazar: "those who have/possess sight." Though "nazar" literally means "sight," it can also mean discrimination. The phrase "Ahl-e-Nazar" means "wise" and also "men who love with discrimination, or love only that which is truly beautiful." The lighter side of the meaning is well covered in the word "connoisseur."

General explanation:

The same strain as in the first two couplets. Bad times have come. There is no honor left in true, idealistic, discriminating love; the lustful also claim to be true lovers, and no scale of value is left to distinguish between the two.

FIFTH COUPLET

General explanation:

The beloved is so beautiful that the lover cannot bear to look at her. Even if she appears, and he tries to look at her, the eyes cannot bear the aspect of the profile; they simply make a kind of halo around it.

Those wild nights have gone forever and with them
The pleasures of sleeping late. I must get up!

I am nothing but dust being blown around in her street;
O wind, let me down, I have no wish to be a bird again.

Look at how gorgeous her footprints are!
Flowers bloom in the slender wake of her walk.

Now that the lechers have taken up beauty
How can we tell them from those who have worshipped for years.

Her face is veiled by my trying to see it;
My shattered sight whirls blindly around her profile.

Mark Strand

GHAZAL
❧ XXX ❧

سایے کی طرح ساتھ پھرین، سرو وصنوبر — تو اس قدِ دلکش سے جو گلزار میں آوے

تب نازِ گرانمایگیِ اشك بجا ہے — جب لختِ جگر، دیدۂ خونبار میں آوے

اُس چشمِ فسونگر کا، اگر پائے، اشارہ — طوطی کی طرح آتے گفتار میں آوے

آتشکدہ ہے سینہ مرا، رازِ نہاں سے — اے وائے اگر معرضِ اظہار میں آوے

گنجینۂ معنی کا طلسم اُس کو سمجھیے — جو لفظ کہ، غالبؔ، مرے اشعار میں آوے

LITERAL TRANSLATION

Like shadows, the pine and the cypress shall walk along your side
If you came into the orchard with this stature that captivates the heart.

Then is the pride in the high worth/value of shedding tears justified
when pieces of the heart come through the eyes that shed (tears of) blood.

If it is commanded by that magician eye (eye that works magic)
The mirror will, like a parrot, begin/learn to speak.

Because of the hidden secrets, my breast abounds with fire;
What may not come to pass if it ever came to manifest expression.

You should consider it the magic of the treasure of meaning,
Any word that comes in my verses.

Form:

Approximately twelve syllables to a line.

SECOND COUPLET

General explanation:

Love is made real only through suffering.

THIRD COUPLET

General explanation:

Two ironies. The parrot can be taught human speech, but it says only what it has been taught—it can only repeat. The magic of her eye is such that the mirror, an inanimate object, will begin to speak; however, like the parrot, it will only say what it has been taught—which is to keep saying that she is beautiful. Mirrors *do* speak. But, unlike the parrot, they only tell the truth and reflect whatever comes in front of them, truthfully. *Her* magic is such that even mirrors can be taught to forego their dispassionate honesty and to keep repeating, like the parrot, whatever she wants to hear.

FOURTH COUPLET

Essential vocabulary:

Āatish-Kadā: Āatish (fire). kadā (place of): place of fire, grate, chimney, furnace, fire-worshippers' temple.

Pine and cypress
would walk with you like your shadows
so would the heart

if you came into the orchard

now a boast of love comes true
the heart bleeds through the eyes

If the eye is a magician
the mirror will speak like a parrot

Secrets
tend the fire in my breast
they would not be fulfilled if revealed

                                                W. S. Merwin

If you appeared
Surely these pines, these solid
Cypresses, would become
water . . . water . . .

Love justified, love made worth its hell?
Tell me more, you who are weighing
Pieces of my heart, floods of my tears

Parrot, parrot mirror, give me back
What she took. I still see her
There. I still see her there, me
Gathering her.

My breast cannot be contained
Something terrible will come of this love
Some terror to both men and women

Any word that is here
came from you, remember
how you dropped it to
me, bending
over

Why fight she says
Why speak I say
We wait, watching to see
Who will break and say
Words of love first

David Ray

GHAZAL
❦ XXXI ❦

نہ شعلے میں یہ کرشمہ، نہ برق میں یہ ادا   کوئی بتاو کہ وہ شوخِ تُند خو کیا ہے؟

جلا ہے جسم جہاں، دل بھی جل گیا ہوگا   کُریدتے ہو جو اب راکھ، جستجو کیا ہے؟

رگوں میں دوڑتے پھرنے کے ہم نہیں قائل   جب آنکھ ہی سے نہ ٹپکا، تو پھر لہو کیا ہے؟

وہ چیز، جس کے لیے ہم کو ہو بہشت عزیز   سوای بادۂ گلفام مُشکبو کیا ہے؟

ہوا ہے شہ کا مُصاحب، پھرے ہے اتراتا   وگرنہ شہر میں غالب کی آبرو کیا ہے؟

LITERAL TRANSLATION

Neither is the flame so miraculous, nor has the lightning such manner/
delicacy;
Somebody tell me what that short-tempered, petulant/capricious one is!

The heart must have been burnt where the body was (burnt)
What is it that you are trying to find in these ashes (now that you look into
the ashes, what is it you are looking for)?

We do not acquiesce simply in running through the veins;
If it does not come to the eyes and run through them, it isn't really blood.

The thing for which we hold (promise of) paradise dear to us
is none other than the rose-colored, musk-odored wine.

He has become/considers himself a friend of the king, now walks around
arrogantly;
Otherwise Ghālib has no other prestige in the city.

Form:

Approximately twelve syllables to a line.

General explanation of the fourth couplet:

Reference to the Muslim promise of a paradise in which there shall be plenty to drink.

Flame is not half so miraculous, nor lightning so delicate;
Who is that spark tempered, petulant, capricious man?

The heart must have burned when the body burned;
What are you looking for in those ashes?

We will not agree merely to run through veins;
If it does not run out of the eyes too, it is not blood.

The very promise of paradise is made dear to us
By the rose-tinted, musk-smelling wine.

Friend to the King, I swaggered about,
Having no other fame in the city.

Thomas Fitzsimmons

Flame is not so wonderful nor has the lightning
such bearing

short-tempered and willful——
what sort of thing would you call it

Where the body was burnt the heart was too
what are you looking for in the ashes

W. S. Merwin

GHAZAL
❧ XXXII ❧

چال، جیسے کڑی کان کا تیر   دل میں ایسے کے،جا کرے کوئی

بات پر واں زبان کٹتی ھے   وہ کہیں اور سنا کرے کوئی

بک رہاموں جنوں میں کیا کیا کچھ   کچھ نہ سمجھے،خدا کرے، کوئی!

کیا کیا خضر نے سکندر سے!   اب کسے رہنما کرے کوئی؟

جب توقع ہی اٹھ گئی، غالب   کیوں کسی کا گلا کرے کوئی؟

LITERAL TRANSLATION

She walks like an arrow released from a tightened bow;
(The challenge is that) one should create a place (for oneself) in the heart
   of one such as her.

On every word (that I utter) she gets ready to cut off the tongue
(She wants that) she should speak, and the other should listen.

I do not know what I am babbling away in my madness;
I hope to God no one understands.

What, after all, Khizer (the mythical prophet who is supposed to have
   known the secret of immortality) did for Alexander (the Greek con-
   queror who sought immortality)!
Whom should one adopt as one's guide?

Ghālib! When all expectations have ended,
Why should one complain about anybody.

Form: Approximately seven syllables to a line.
No explanation necessary.

Her walk is an arrow, zap at a target—
that you could find a place in a heart like hers!

You offer a word, she slashes the tongue:
she is the speaker; others may listen.

(Whatever I'm babbling so recklessly on,
for God's sake let no one out there understand!)

Alexander the Great was made a fool of,
hailed as immortal, before he died.

Ghalib! Why expect to know where to turn?
Hopes die. You know that. How can you complain?

William Stafford

GHAZAL
❧ XXXIII ❧

اُس بزم میں مجھے نہیں بنتی حیا کیسے   بیٹھا رہا، اگرچہ اشارے ہوا کیسے

رکھنا پھروں ہوں، خرقہ و سجادہ رہنِ مَے   مدت ہوئی ہے، دعوتِ آب و ہوا کیسے

مقدور ہو، تو خاک سے پوچھوں کہ اے لئیم   تونے وہ گنجہای گرانمایہ کیا کیے؟

صحبت میں غیر کی نہ پڑی ہو، کہیں، یہ خو؟   دینے لگا ہے بوسہ، بغیر التجا کیے

ضد کی ہے اور بات، مگر خو بری نہیں   بھولے سے اُس نے سینکڑوں وعدے وفا کیے

LITERAL TRANSLATION

In this gathering, I can have no shame (cannot act out of mere self-respect);
I kept sitting, although fingers were pointed at me.

For my wine, I am pawning my ragged garment and my prayer rug;
It is long since we drank in an open banquet.

If it were ordained for me (if I were lucky enough to), I would question this earth, saying: you, who are avaricious (miserly)!
What did you do with all those treasures of great worth?

She must have surely picked up this new habit in the company of others;
She has started giving kisses without entreaties.

Intransigence/stubbornness is another thing. Otherwise, she is not ill-natured (her true nature is not bad);
Even out of forgetfulness, she has kept many of her promises.

Form:

Approximately twelve syllables to a line.

FIRST COUPLET

General explanation:

Obsessed lover. Has lost even his self-respect. He is unwanted in the company of his beloved and her friends, and knows it; but adoration has made him so abject that he cannot go away even if everyone makes fun of him.

SECOND COUPLET

Essential vocabulary:

Kharqā: ragged garment of a devotee, mendicant, etc.

Sajjādā: The rug or carpet on which Muslims worship.

THIRD COUPLET

General explanation:

As in the opening couplet of Ghazal XV, Ghālib thinks of the great, the beautiful who have died as great treasures buried in the ground, and wonders what happened to them once they were buried. The earth is symbolized as a miserly fellow who keeps his treasures hidden.

FOURTH COUPLET

General explanation:

That the conquest has become easier, and that the beloved is now more flirtatious, shows that she has been in bad company; virtue has become less fastidious, easier.

FIFTH COUPLET

General explanation:

Bit of verbal jugglery here. The second line means: although she always remembers *not* to keep her promises, her good nature makes her forget the resolve; she keeps the promises, some of them at any rate, despite herself.

Here, I am without shame;
Let them point, I remain.

Rags and prayer rug I have pawned for wine;
So long since openly we drank at banquet.

Could I, I would challenge earth itself, asking:
"Miser, where have you hidden all that vast treasure?"

Among strangers she learned a new habit:
She kisses without being begged.

Stubborn, yes, but not altogether ill natured:
In moments of forgetfulness she even keeps promises.

Thomas Fitzsimmons

Everybody looking but it makes no difference
I just sit still and let them point.

Pawn my rags and prayer rug for wine.
A long time since it was offered at a table.

If fate permitted I would say to the earth: Miser
what did you do with all those priceless things?

She must have picked up this habit from somebody else,
giving kisses now before she's asked.

But determination is something else. She's not spiteful.
She's kept many promises out of sheer forgetfulness.

W. S. Merwin

Why did you come here
if not to bear that terrible
aftermath of complacency
a quiet kitchen
an autumn
as well as the explosion
of first our hands
then our hair

We have been the most fantastic
places together
yet we sit here like children
saying 'are you sure you like me?'
sitting cross-legged, toying
with each other's hair

The tricks of her mouth are suddenly changed
Surely she has learned something from others
Suddenly she is able to give without being asked
suddenly she is asking

She must be a generous woman
giving so much
not even trying, even once or twice
keeping promises

Just because fingers pointed at me
was I really supposed to get up
and no longer sit at your side
no longer go with you
to our special places, bearing
our own light through the shadows   *David Ray*

I had no shame. I went to her party.
She and her friends laughed at me and I just sat there.

To buy wine I pawned my old coat and my prayer rug;
It's been a long time since we drank together.

If I were chosen to ask the earth questions,
I would ask why does it withhold its most valuable treasures.

She has picked up some habits from her new friends;
She gives away kisses without batting an eye.

Stubbornness is something else. She is not bad-natured.
She will try to break promises, forget, and end up keeping them.

Mark Strand

GHAZAL

❦ XXXIV ❦

غیر پھرتا ہے لیے یوں ترے خط کو کہ اگر

کوئی پوچھے کہ ، یہ کیا ہے؟، تو چھپائے نہ بنے

اس نزاکت کا برا ہو؛ وہ بھلے ہیں، تو کیا؟

ہاتھ آویں، تو اُنہیں ہاتھ لگائے نہ بنے

موت کی راہ نہ دیکھوں؟ کہ بن آئے نہ رہے

تم کو چاہوں؟ کہ نہ آؤ، تو بُلائے نہ بنے

کہ سکے کون کہ یہ جلوہ گری کس کی ہے؟

پردہ چھوڑا ہے وہ اُس نے کہ اُٹھائے نہ بنے

عشق پر زور نہیں، ہے یہ وہ آتش، غالب

کہ لگائے نہ لگے، اور بُجھائے نہ بنے ۱

LITERAL TRANSLATION

The other (your other lover/my enemy) is going around with your letter in such a way (so openly)
That he may not even conceal it if someone were to ask him what it was.

Although she is good/amiable, her elegant tenderness is such
that I would be afraid to touch her even if she were to come close/even if she allowed me to touch her.

Death is so certain that it will come anyway, whether I wait for her or not;
And, my love for you? So that, if you don't come, I can't even send for you.

Who can say as to whose vision it is;
Such a curtain He has put between us that I cannot lift (it).

Ghālib! I have no power over love; It is a fire
That I can neither light, nor put out.

Form:

Approximately twelve syllables to a line.

FIRST COUPLET

General explanation:

In other words, your other lover is looking for people who would
ask him about the letter, and he would immediately read out the
whole letter to them. Source of shame for Ghālib.

SECOND COUPLET

General explanation:

She is so beautiful, so delicately wrought that I would be reluctant
to touch her, for fear of defiling her. This is an extent of verbal
wit that I cannot even begin to explain.

THIRD COUPLET

General explanation:

Inevitability of death and lack of desire for it, played against de-
sire to ask the beloved to come. The helplessness of love. Respect
for her own decisions.

FOURTH COUPLET

General explanation:

Mystical verse. God hides Himself and cannot be known with any
kind of specific knowledge.

They say that other one goes carrying your letters
so openly that if asked he has to confess the writer.

So delicate is her goodness, so tenderly wrought
that were she to melt into my hands, I dare not touch her.

Death will come at last, whether I want it or not;
I can't help calling for you, though you will never come.

Who can say to whom the vision belongs?
The curtain He has drawn is too heavy to pull aside.

Ghalib! love is a fire that lights itself
and dies out of itself, beyond our wills.

Adrienne Rich

The other fellow is wearing her letter, flaunting it
so he can pretend to hide it.

She is so generous but high-toned that I'd reach, then
shrink, even if she came rubbing around like the others.

Sure as death—it'll come, whether or no—
I dread her presence but can't help courting it.

What a puzzle, this having-and-not-having!
There's a veil; there are thoughts I can't fathom.

Ghalib! I can't contend with love. It's a fire
so dead I can't light it, so hot I can't put it out.

William Stafford

GHAZAL

❧ XXXV ❧

دیا ہے دل اگر اُس کو، بشر ہے، کیا کہیے؟

ہوا رقیب، تو ہوہ نامہ بر ہے، کیا کہیے؟

بہ ضد کہ آج نہ آوے، اور آے بن نہ رہے

قضا سے شکوہ، میں کس قدر ہے، کیا کہیے؟

سمجھہ کے کرتے ہیں بازار میں، وہ، پرسشِ حال

کہ یہ کہے کہ ”سر رہگزر ہے، کیا کہیے؟،

اُنہیں سوال پہ زعمِ جنوں ہے، کیوں لڑیے؟

میں جواب سے قطعِ نظر ہے، کیا کہیے؟

کہا ہے کس نے کہ غالب برا نہیں؟ لیکن

سوای اس کے کہ آشفتہ سر ہے، کیا کہیے؟‘

LITERAL TRANSLATION

If he has given his heart to her, he too is human; there is nothing you can say.

Even if he has become your rival, he is still your messenger; there is nothing you can say.

She (death) is adamant that it will not come today, but that she certainly will come;

I cannot say how many complaints I have against death.

She takes care to inquire after our condition only in public;
Knowing that I will say that it is a public place and cannot go into
  detail.

Whenever we entreat/beg/ask, she claims we are mad. Why quarrel?
We are not interested in the answer. What can we say?

Who has said that Ghālib is not bad; but,
Except that he is mad, what else can you say?

Form:

  Approximately twelve syllables to a line.

FIRST COUPLET

General explanation:

  What has happened is rather interesting. There was a man whom
  Ghālib had employed as a messenger to his beloved; unfortunately,
  the messenger fell in love with the same woman. In view of the
  beloved's great beauty, Ghālib recognizes this reaction on the
  part of the messenger as perfectly human. What makes the situa-
  tion worse, however, is that Ghālib still depends on him for his
  own contact with the young lady. Worse still, the messenger has
  greater opportunity to meet her, and therefore to plead his own
  case, than Ghālib. I wonder what I would do in Ghālib's place?

SECOND COUPLET

General explanation:

  On the one hand, death is inevitable; on the other, she will not
  come today when we are so sad and *want* her to come. Our first
  complaint is that she will not grant us immortality, second that
  we cannot choose the moment of her arrival.

FOURTH COUPLET

Essential vocabulary:

Zoam-e-Junoon: zoam (claim of strength or power), Junoon (insanity/madness). Claiming that someone is mad. Thus, the reading of the line would be: 'Even while asking the question, she already claims that I am mad; what is the point even in trying to argue?'

Qatai-e-Nazar: Qatai (to cut, cut away, take away), Nazar (sight). To ignore, overlook. Not to take interest. To know what the answer would be, therefore, not even to argue.

FIFTH COUPLET

Essential vocabulary:

Āashuftā-Sar: Āashuftā (scattered, distracted, disordered), Sar (head). Literally, scatter-headed, distracted (in a sense, scatter-brained, but not altogether), insane.

If he fell in love with her that was only human
        you can't blame him
        and he still carries your messages to her
        you can't scold him

Death says she'll come
        but not today when I want her
        one more thing I have against her

She's careful to ask how I am
        in public
        where I can't tell her

When she asks she says I'm mad
        why answer
        and with the answer itself
        not worth making

                                    W. S. Merwin

GHAZAL
❦ XXXVI ❦

باز يحۂ اطفـال ﮨﮯ، دنيـا، مرے آگے

موتـا ﮨﮯ شب و روز تماشا مرے آگے

اك كهبل ﮨﮯ، اور نگ سليماں،مرے نزديك

اك بات ﮨﮯ، اعجـاز مسيحا، مرے آگے

پهر ديكهـﮯ انداز گل افشـانئ گفتار

ركه دے كوئ پيانة صها مرے آگے

ايماں مجهـﮯ روكے ﮨﮯ، جو كهينچے ﮨﮯ مجهـﮯ كفر

كعبه مرے پيچهـﮯ ﮨﮯ، كليسا مرے آگے

گو هاته كو جنبش نہيں، آنكهوں ميں تو دم ﮨﮯ

رهنے دو ابهى سـاغر و مينا مرے آگے

LITERAL TRANSLATION

This world is a children's playground for me.
This spectacle unfolds day and night in front of my eyes.

A (child's) play is the throne of Solomon for me;
An ordinary thing is the miracle of the Messiah in my eyes.

Then you should see the manner of the flow of conversation—
Let someone place the goblet and the wine jug in front of me.

Faith stops me, if impiety pulls me toward itself;
Kā'bā is behind me, the church in front of me.

Though the hands cannot move, the eyes at least have life;
Let the jug of wine and the goblet stay in front of me.

Form:

Approximately twelve syllables to a line.

THIRD COUPLET

Comment:

The comparison between the flow of wine and the flow of conversation is interesting.

FOURTH COUPLET

Essential vocabulary:

Kufr: Impiety, infidelity, idolatry, paganism, blasphemy.

General explanation:

Stresses of belief, temptations to give up Faith. It is interesting that Christianity should be mentioned as providing the temptations of non-belief, paganism, etc.

To me this world is a children's playground

> Solomon's throne a toy
> the miracle of the Messiah
> a handle in the kitchen

> just put wine in front of me
> and listen

> if Faith pulls at my sleeve Impiety
> pulls better
> keep the wine there

> even when the hands have stopped moving
> there's life in the eyes

W. S. Merwin

Since I began ogling colors in dime stores
all manners of toys and baubles
I have been ecstatic. It is like
other habits I learned slowly, then sped up

The Messiah would mean nothing to me
To the throne of Solomon for his latest
victory or crowning
I would send reporters
You're the only face that stops me blind
with faith. I'd split the earth
that let you walk away on her

As I said, move nothing, not even your hands
Let the jug and the wine stay equally silent
While we hear our dark breath
        becoming darker together

David Ray

GHAZAL

❧ XXXVII ❧

مزاروں خواہشیں ایسی کہ ہر خواہش پہ دم نکلے

بہت نکلے مرے ارمان، لیکن پھر بھی کم نکلے

نکلنا خلد سے آدم کا سنتے آے ہیں، لیکن

بہت بے آبرو ہوکر، ترے کوچے سے ہم نکلے

ہوئی اس دور میں منسوب مجھ سے، بادہ آشائی

پھر آیا وہ زمانہ، جو جہاں میں جامِ جم نکلے

ہوئی جن سے توقع خستگی کی داد پانے کی

وہ ہم سے بھی زیادہ خستۂ تیغِ ستم نکلے

LITERAL TRANSLATION

There are a thousand such desires that each would require an entire lifetime;
Many of my wishes have been gratified but even those many were too few
(fewer than I wish were gratified, not enough).

We have always heard of Adam leaving (being made to leave) the primal
paradise, but
I was much (less literally, more) disgraced when I left (was made to leave)
your abode.

Drinking (drunkenness) has been associated with my name in this period;
Once more, an era has arrived (begun) in which Jamshed's cup should
appear.

Whenever we expected someone to appreciate our weaknesses (failures),
He was found to be more wounded (killed, deadened) by the sword of cruelties (hard times, misfortunes).

O preacher! Do not, for God's sake, lift the curtain of the Kā'bā.
Maybe the same unbelieving idol is found (appears) here as well.

Form:

Each line of approximately fourteen syllables. In terms of stresses, we could compare it to the iambic foot.

FIRST COUPLET
Essential vocabulary:

Dam Niklai: Very colloquial. Literally, would lose breath, or life. Losing something that is vital to life, something that would take a whole life-span. No literal translation which could make any sense in English is possible.

Armān: Wish, longing, etc.

SECOND COUPLET
Essential vocabulary:

Khuld: One of the several words for paradise, or the heavens.

Bai-Ābru: Bai is a negative prefix, meaning a lack of something, in this case "abru." Ābru—literally, brightness of face; honor, respect, dignity, repute.

Koochā: Street, the area in which one's house is situated. Abode, for which I have compromised, may be useless, besides being inaccurate as it is.

THIRD COUPLET
Essential vocabulary:

Daur: Period, era. The word, in a different and appropriate context, also means "a round of drinks." My guess is that Ghālib is playing on this other meaning of the word.

B⁻dā-Āshāmi: To be in the habit, or grip, of drinking. Addicted.

Zamānā: Era. Extremely interesting etymology. "Zāmān" is "the world;" "Zamana" is that which encompasses it; hence, time. But differentiated from "waqt" (Time) by defining a certain length of it; hence, era.

Jamshaid: Persian king, mythically known to have possessed a cup in which he could see the reflection of future events.

FOURTH COUPLET
Essential vocabulary:

Khastagi: Weakness, physical and moral, that results from having failed, fatigue, brittleness, moral weariness, the feeling of having grown old, sense of failure, having been thoroughly consumed by the sheer effort of a doomed mission.

FIFTH COUPLET *
General explanation:

The poet is indulging in all kinds of allusions and word-play. The phrase "for God's sake" is used as an emphatic exclamation, as we all commonly use it; it is also used literally: for the sake of God, in seeking God. The poet is also making use of a few historical facts: that the Kā'bā, the grand shrine where Muslims from all over

---

* This couplet is not found in Arshi's edition of the Urdu *Deevan*. I had seen it elsewhere and had considered it authentic. More recently, I have discovered that the couplet had been composed by Bahadur Shah Zafar, the last Moghul king and had been corrected and improved by Ghālib. I was obviously misled by the mark Ghālib's improvement has left on the couplet.

the world congregate for their annual pilgrimage, was in fact a temple for idol-worship before the advent of Islam; that at the heart of the shrine is still a huge stone, wrapped in beautifully embroidered cloth, which is supposedly holy.

The Urdu words for unbelieving ("Kāfir") and idol ("Sanam") are often used in poetry for the beloved.

The poet and the preacher are traditional adversaries in Urdu poetics, the latter being the symbol of total ignorance regarding love, life, and religion.

Of my thousand cravings, each one a career,
many I've done, but never enough.

You've heard of Adam driven weeping from Eden—
worse, leaving your place I felt you-forsaken.

Drink, for a spell, tarnished my name.
Even a king once found some truth in the cup.

Just when you think someone may feel for your plight,
it turns out he's worse off—even calloused, maybe.

For God's sake, preacher, don't snoop the wrong temple.
You might stumble on something better neglected.

William Stafford

There are a thousand desires like this, each needing a lifetime.
Of my wishes, many were gratified, but far from enough.

We have heard of Adam driven from paradise.
My fall from grace was far worse, when I left where you live.

At this time they couple my name with drunkenness.
One more age has dawned that needs Jamshed's cup.

Each time we expected sympathy for our failings
the blade of disaster fell, and we were found near death.

Oh preacher, for God's sake do not raise the Kaa'ba's curtain.
It may hide one more idol in which there can be no belief.

W. S. Merwin

INDEX OF CONTRIBUTORS
AND FIRST LINES

Mark Strand